CONTACT ME

SPEAKING

HIRE ME FOR YOUR NEXT EVENT

WWW.TODAYYOUCHOOSE.COM

SOCIAL

 WWW.TODAYYOUCHOOSE.COM

 JASON@JASONMARTINGROUP.COM

 WWW.FACEBOOK.COM/JASON.D.MARTIN.5

 WWW.INSTAGRAM.COM/JASON.D.MARTIN.5

JASON MARTIN

PRAISE FOR

THIS IS YOUR CAPTAIN SPEAKING

"*This is Your Captain Speaking* is a dedication to life, family, and the pursuit of being truly alive. It's a story about what endures: the lessons we fight to learn and the ones we are destined to pass on. With humor and abiding love, Martin's words remind us to dream big, feel deeply, and savor the extraordinary gift of a human life."

—ABBY MASLIN, Author, Educator

"Every day is a gift that we must not take for granted. Tomorrow is tomorrow, but today has the possibility to provide a lifelong memory. As a father and husband, Jason doesn't want to miss a single precious moment, *This Is Your Captain Speaking* is a legacy for his family that they will cherish for many years to come."

—MARK BATTERSON,
New York Times best selling author of *The Circle Maker*,
Lead Pastor of National Community Church

"They say you should change your job or your course in life a few times during your working years. Jason has done that and forged his way to success through honesty, integrity, hard work, and support from his family. In this book, you'll find some great lessons on how to succeed . . . and do it the RIGHT way."

—ERIC WATERS, Head Athletic Trainer, Utah Jazz

"As Jason's longtime business coach, I've grown to know an exceptionally positive, successful, and driven business-man. Our weekly conversations center around business. However, in reading Jason's book, Jason reveals the 'real' man in business(man). He touches on the important side of his motivation to succeed. His 'big why' if you will. That 'why' is literally a common thread throughout the book. We all have a 'big why,' but some folks don't know how to iden-tify it themselves. There's no ambiguity in this book, Jason's catalysts to living life are here for all to see. Being a father myself, I can so relate to Jason's experience with the world and kids. It's obvious that great values start with a parent(s). And of course, I learned a few other revelations from Jason's book. . . . I never knew Jason was a 'doctor' or a 'meteo-rologist' either . . . lol . . . Most of us wish to have a lasting legacy of our journey through life, memorializing that for the future. Jason has done just that . . . I'm anxious to read volume two as Jason continues to live a life worth living."

—GLEEN NEELY, Fortune 50 Business Consultant

"*This Is Your Captain Speaking* is a beautiful ode to the privilege of fatherhood. Martin's book provides a moral compass for his family and reminds parents not to wait too long to express to their children the lessons and love for one has for them. His gorgeous recounting of the journeys he has had in life with his children is delightful, honest, and fulfilling to read. The subtleties of his personal relationship with each child and his reflection as a father warm you from the inside out. The lessons learned, the miles traveled, and the inspiration of being a father. Martin writes so dearly to his family and inspires me to want to do the same."

—Azul Terronez, Author of *The Art of Apprenticeship*

"Over the years I've gotten to know Jason Martin, Super Realtor, then Super Friend, now Super Dad. This is a fun and uplifting read. It not only gives the reader insight into the Martin Express but also shares some real gold nuggets for life. What's on your precious memory wall?"

—Doug Brock, Colonel, United States Air Force

THIS IS YOUR CAPTAIN SPEAKING

THIS IS YOUR CAPTAIN SPEAKING

Life Lessons from the Journey So Far

JASON MARTIN

Published by Mandala Tree Press
https://mandalatreepress.com/

Paperback ISBN: 978-1-954801-00-4
Hardcover ISBN: 978-1-954801-02-8
Ebook ISBN: 978-1-954801-01-1

SEL016000 SELF-HELP / Personal Growth / Happiness

Cover design by Lisa Barbee
Edited by Melissa Miller
Typeset by Kaitlin Barwick

www.todayyouchoose.com

To my family Connor, Isabella, Riley, and Jennifer.
I cherish the memories we create together.
I love you to infinity and beyond.

CONTENTS

CONTENTS

CHAPTER 1

DEAR KIDS

D EAR KIDS,
There is so much I want you to teach you about life.
Life is so precious. Time is slipping away, but I want you
to know that I capture every moment I can, even when
you have no idea I am. You are growing up so fast: a day
goes by in a matter of seconds; a year feels more like a
long weekend.

Someone once shared with me that being a parent is
like flying a kite: you hold on tight, then slowly let out a
little more string until the kite takes flight. Truth be told,
Mom and I don't want to let the string out yet. We want
to hold on as long as we can. Despite this, we realize we
have to let the string out. We understand that one day
you will fly on your own, and we want you to soar!

Life is about living in the moment, but the memories
we have created will forever be a part of my life. Our
memories together are the greatest moments of my life!
When you were born, something very strange happened
to me that words can't describe. Other dads have tried to
explain this out-of-body experience, but you don't fully

understand it until it happens. My entire world changed the day you guys entered this world.

One day I will leave this earth, as we all do, and this book shall serve as a reminder of who Dad was: my beliefs, my priorities, and my core values. I am perfectly imperfect—as we all are. I am proud, I am humble, I am grateful, I am a husband, and, above all else, I am a dad. I know this letter sounds like I am writing from my deathbed, but I am not. I am SO alive, and I am full of life.

We are each on our own unique journey in this world, and this part of my journey has been very special. I don't ever want to leave behind our memories together. While this book is for you, it's also for me so I can hold onto the kite forever.

Living a full life is about becoming the best version of yourself possible. As selfish as that sounds, it's not about me—it's about you guys. I know that by becoming the best version of myself possible, those closest to me will reap the benefits.

Life is not and will not always be easy. Through adversity, I have chosen to come out a stronger man. Use your low points in life as an opportunity. You are going to fail many times in your life, but you only truly fail if you don't get back up.

Love makes the world a better place. The most important cup you can fill up in life is those living under your own roof. Leave the world a better place than you found it. Our world is filled with good people and bad people, but there are definitely more good than bad, and even those who seem evil to their core might one day surprise you. Give people a chance. Don't predetermine who you think they are.

Don't look back on your life with regrets, even though you will make mistakes. Always be true to yourself. Don't let the world decide your path. Trust in what God is telling you. To hear what he is saying, you must listen. Be calm, slow down, be grateful, and enjoy the moment. All we have in life are moments in time and memories. Happiness will come from being present in the moment.

Always be filled with hope. Never remove the word *hope* from your vocabulary or mind. Always be a student; your brain will thank you. Your body is your temple, so take care of it. Try new things—like writing a book.

This book is filled with the memories we have created together and the lessons I want you to keep with you long after I am gone from this earth. I don't ever want you to wonder "what would Dad do" or "what would Dad say": it's all in here.

This is your captain speaking. "Mom and I love you kids more than anything in the world. You have given us our greatest sense of joy and purpose. May your kites drift in and out of the highest clouds on the perfect day."

—Love, Dad

(For those reading who are outside of the Martin family circle of trust, I call myself the captain because when we go on family trips, I cusp my hand over my mouth to create the sound of a microphone and introduce myself as the captain. I am the captain of our ship, which happens to be a minivan, and the name of our ship is the *Martin Express*. Welcome aboard!)

In the following chapters, we are going to embark on a journey together where I will introduce you to my family (my crewmates). Our journey together will take us through perfect days and storms alike. These experiences have become my life compass.

CHAPTER 2

RILEY

ANYONE WHO KNOWS me will tell you that above all else comes my family. This is a generational gift that has been passed down from my mom (a.k.a., Grandma Martin), who has had quite a profound impact on my life. My mom didn't teach this concept to my sister and me; she led by example. My sister, Lisa, and I never questioned Mom's love for us! Thanks to Grandma Martin, I don't cherish anything more in life than my own family. If I succeed as a father and a husband, then mission accomplished. That's it. It's that simple for me. My greatest moments in life have come from the memories I have created with my family.

I asked our youngest daughter, Riley, what she thought I should write about in this book. Without hesitation, she said, "ME." Well, Riley, I named this chapter after you!

Our living room wall is filled with pictures from fun family adventures, like our three-week West Coast trip to California, our annual trip to New York during the holidays, spring break cruises, and pumpkin patches. We are a very lucky family indeed, and I don't take our time together for granted. Our living room wall is a storybook of our lives together. I try so hard to capture the memories—you know, those moments in time that you will never get back again. While you may never get the cherished moments back again, you can and should be on the lookout for the next one.

Yesterday, after weeks of lobbying from all three of you kids, Mom and I caved, and we ordered a full-size circus-like trampoline. For the record, I consider trampolines to be very dangerous. However, thanks to COVID-19, we were open to anything that might entertain you guys. When the trampoline arrived, I was certain it would take days to put together and that Mom and I would want a divorce by the time we were done working on it together. I usually struggle with directions, which frustrates Mom, who occasionally tosses a few curse words my way. However, thanks to a little help from YouTube and a set of easy-to-understand instructions, we pulled it off without a hitch (marriage saved!). This was a sign of good things to come.

With red faces and sweat dripping everywhere on a humid ninety-degree day, you kids were as happy as you could be. Who knew a trampoline could bring such joy? You jumped for at least ten straight hours, with an occasional break for a quick dip in the pool to cool off. Jump then swim, jump then swim, all day long! The excitement of floating through the air had you children giggling well into the evening. It was pure joy, it was pure fun. Summertime fun is the best, but to me it can be more than just fun. It can become a cherished moment.

As I was relaxing on the outdoor couch by the pool around 7:00 p.m., watching the three of you jump on the trampoline together, I realized something: it was one of those cherished moments you want to hold onto forever. Riley looked like a frog flying high into the night sky as the older kids popcorned her—bouncing on the trampoline in a way that makes someone go flying into the air like a popcorn kernel. All three of you children were soaring. The sensation of flying made you children ecstatic. I am so glad we opted for the trampoline (with perimeter netting). The three of you were living your best lives in the moment and just being kids. The thing is, I am very aware of time. I am aware those moments won't last forever.

As I was comfortably appreciating the moment from the couch, my mind and body were at peace. I was filled with such gratitude and love, fully realizing I am a lucky man. I was in my own state of zen and could have easily drifted off for a quick cat nap, something a parent of three rarely gets an opportunity to do.

Suddenly, the three amigos started to chant: "Bounce us, bounce us, bounce us!" I already told you how comfortable I was on the couch. The last thing I wanted to do was get my heart rate up by jumping on the trampoline. One of my nicknames is Old Man Martin, because around 7:00 p.m. I usually have on my PJs and prefer to be asleep no later than 10:00 p.m. The kids usually have no interest in honoring my early bedtime wishes. Their chant grew louder and louder until I caved. We jumped together for about an hour until I was also fully drenched in sweat and could feel my legs burning. Jumping on a trampoline with three kids is quite a cardio workout, but it was totally worth it!

The temperature was perfect. A full moon began to surface, and the pool glowed from the party lights we had put up last summer. It was a magical moment, just me and the kids having fun without a care in the world! That's the exact type of memory that I hope I will cherish forever. That's what I live for!

In an effort to capture those special moments in time I began journaling. I started journaling about eight years ago, and I wish I had started sooner. Jen and I had a conversation recently where we asked each other this question: If the house was on fire and you could only grab one thing, what would it be? Of course, in our scenario the kids and Scooby the dog were already safe. You already know my answer: the journal. Not a single possession is more valuable than my journal filled with memories. Jen said she would grab the boxes filled with pictures.

When you leave the earth, what will you leave behind? I believe the most valuable gift won't be wealth, but memories. Memories filled with love. Life will pass you by completely if you don't slow down long enough to capture the memories. Make your family your top priority. I am certain it's something you will not regret.

Yesterday I decided to read this chapter to Riley to see what my audience might think of my work. Guess what she said? "Dad, you didn't even talk about me that much." Well, Riley, just about the entire book is about you, Connor, and Izzy, but I think I understand what you are looking for.

Riley is full of life. She wakes up every day filled with excitement and ready to have fun! Riley loves playing, fashion, lipstick, jumping on the trampoline, sweets, riding her bike, and (while she won't admit it) playing the piano. She always has a smile on her face, and she is a pure optimist. Her excitement, passion for life, and laughs are the best. May you always remain our little girl. Mom and I love you very much, blondie.

I already know what my other two children are thinking right now. What about me? What about my chapter? I'm going to let you in on a little secret: just like Christmas where you each get the same number of presents, you are each mentioned the same number of times in this book!

CHAPTER 3

MEET THE GANG

I WOULD LIKE TO share with you a few things you should know about my kids. My wife, Jen, and I have three children. Connor and Isabella (age thirteen) are twins, and our youngest daughter is Riley (age nine). Riley is our fashionista. Her first full sentence in life was telling someone, "I like your shoes." It sounds like I am joking, but I am not. She has more dresses than you can imagine. Most children want toys for Christmas, but Riley prefers dresses!

When Riley was five years old, we took a family trip to Disneyland. I don't think anyone in our family was more excited to visit Disneyland than Riley. All of her favorite princesses awaited. On this particular day, the temps were in the nineties, the air was heavy, and it was a total steam bath. Our shirts were soaked with sweat and much like all the fluids in my body, my wallet was about to be drained.

I now fully understand why Disney is the profit machine that it is. After paying the equivalent of a mortgage payment just to enter the park, they then come after your retirement income. As soon as you enter the park, a princess store awaits! My five-year-old princess noticed this store immediately—a very strategic play by Disney. In less than five minutes, we were at the register for the first time. Do you have any doubt what Riley wanted to buy? A princess dress, of course—a princess dress that might be more expensive than some wedding dresses! Of course we purchased the dress and, despite the bubbling temps, Riley wore her princess dress the entire day.

I have no idea where Riley developed this love for fashion. My wife, Jen, prefers jeans and a T-shirt. . . . I prefer shorts, T-shirt, and a pair of crocs. Riley has become my fashion consultant. She will go into my closet and choose my outfit for the day. Her selections are usually spot on! Riley is full of life, always happy, and most of the time dressed for a good time. Some of her favorite footwear includes her black fur boots and her sparkly high heels. She doesn't just sport her favorite footwear on special occasions—this is what she wears when going outside to play. She's a fashionista. How she doesn't break her tiny ankles while running in heels is a mystery to me. If Riley doesn't work in the fashion industry, I will be very surprised. Riley is also a lover and cuddler, and she still likes to sleep in mom and dad's bed.

Our middle child, Isabella, has the biggest heart you can imagine. She's our middle child because her twin brother arrived in the world two minutes earlier, which he's happy to remind her about if she ever happens to forget. Isabella—a.k.a., Izzy—has a heart of gold and is always thinking about others. She's been attending mission trips with our church since age ten. She loves church youth group and is definitely the spiritual leader of our household. Izzy always wants to help those less fortunate, including those in her own school. One afternoon, Izzy came home and shared a story that had my heart weeping. It was about a middle schooler nicknamed Rat Girl. Middle schoolers can be ruthless; what a terrible nickname!

Rat Girl shared with Izzy that her family didn't have enough money to get her a haircut. Apparently Rat Girl also smelled a little bit and was made fun of. You know who didn't make fun of Rat Girl? My Izzy, who was heartbroken when she heard her story. That night Izzy and I went out looking for a gift card to a hair salon!

Isabella loves reading, her family, soccer, and, at her core, she cares for people. She also has a passion for entrepreneurship—more on that later. I can't wait to see the path Izzy chooses in life, but I am certain whatever path she chooses, giving will always be a part of her plan. Love you, Izzy.

Connor, my man, is my number-one dude! As you already know, he's the oldest (by two minutes <:) of our three children. He loves hearing that, because his twin sister, Izzy, is taller than him at the moment. Don't worry, Connor. You will one day be taller than your twin sister.

Connor has fire in his belly, and when he makes his mind up to do something, it's on. He won't be denied. He is currently training for a triathlon because he wants to be in better shape for the upcoming hockey season. He has every intention of playing in the NHL. To keep him active, Jen and I decided to build a sport-court for hockey in our backyard. On any given day, Connor might spend six to ten hours on the court working on his game. He's out there seven days a week. He eats, sleeps, and breathes hockey! His drive and will to succeed are amazing. I tapped on his bedroom door recently to see what he was up to. Naturally, he was doing sit ups to strengthen his core for hockey.

Connor needs to be in motion; sitting still is not in his DNA. Connor's motor is going from the time he wakes until the time he passes out. Many nights, long after I have slipped into my pajamas, Connor still has energy to burn. He recently needed my presence on the sport-court as a hockey defender so he could work on his new move called the Kutcheroff. Don't ask me to explain what a Kutcheroff is, but I happily played my role in my pajamas. I play with him as much as I can, but there are plenty of days when my entire body is stiff the next day from trying to keep up with him. Whatever path he chooses in life, he will be a huge success as long as it's something he's passionate about. His all-in approach is going to take him far in life! Love you, pal!

From here on out, at the end of each chapter of this book, I will be sharing a life lesson with you. These are the lessons I have learned from my years on this earth that I want to share with you. This section will be called The Lesson.

THE LESSON

I added this chapter to the book not only to give you a glimpse into the Martin household but also as a reference point for my kids so they never forget who they are. You should always be yourself. Don't let the world or other people define who you are.

As you grow older, you might change your perspective or take a different path, but who you are at your core is defined early on. Stay true to who you are. Always strive to be a better version of yourself, but stay true to yourself. Don't let the world define you. Happiness is achieved through authenticity. Mom and Dad want you to be happy, but you need to define what that looks like for you. If you are happy, we will support whatever that looks like as long as it's true to you! Pursue your passions!

CHAPTER 4

SCOOBY

S COOBY THE DOG is the sixth member of the Martin family. He is a black Australian labradoodle who loves sleeping in our bed. In fact, Scooby prefers *my* pillow and *my* side of the bed. He would prefer I sleep in a different location altogether so he can have my spot. Early each morning, before the sun rises, I head downstairs to let Scooby out for his morning bathroom break. He doesn't stay outside long; he takes care of business quickly so that he can get back to his warm spot in my bed. As he re-enters the house after his morning bathroom break, he races up the stairs so I have no chance of claiming his spot on my pillow! I am not exaggerating. He doesn't even acknowledge my presence as he sprints back in the door.

Scooby is a soft, cuddly, gentle creature who loves to give hugs. Literally, he lifts his two front paws in the air and then wraps them around your waist. He holds on tight and might be the best hugger in the family. Our whole family loves hugs, cuddles, and foot rubs. Scooby prefers the belly rub over the foot rub, but he will take whatever love you throw his way. He also likes hiding shoes, eating food from the trash can, and taking long naps in the beanbag next to the warm fire.

Scooby has a few nicknames, but our favorite is Mister Furry. Mister Furry is convinced that he is human. Scooby is tortured daily by the Martin family, but primarily by Riley. He is regularly transformed into a variety of different characters. She is convinced that he is one of her baby dolls. On any given day, he could be the Easter Bunny or a reindeer. He is also Riley's favorite pillow and her preferred model for her latest fashion design. He is often covered entirely in blankets (I am not sure how he breathes) as the kids find it hysterical to hide him. If he's not being covered in blankets, then he might be role playing as a horse. Yep, poor Scooby is absolutely tortured daily but he loves the attention.

Mister Furry can be a P-I-T-A at times, but we love him to death. P-I-T-A is a code word the Martin family uses for someone who is being a pain in the a--. When he's really hungry, he waits for the perfect opportunity to climb onto our dinner table when no one is looking, helping himself to a few leftovers. In desperate times he's willing to dig through the trash. He has figured out how to use his paws to open the trash can lid. Despite a few character flaws (we all have them), Scooby is the most patient member of the Martin family. He takes life in stride, very rarely getting angry about anything unless you're trying to move him from my bed. He's willing to put up with a lot, but if he's in my bed and you try to move him, you will see his teeth.

Quick sidenote: I read this chapter to my family to see what they might think. They loved it, which made me very happy. However, they were concerned someone might call animal control on us. Please understand that Scooby is well loved and, in fact, adores all the attention. He loves us and we love him. We would never do anything to harm Mister Furry, so please don't call animal control on us. This paragraph brought to you by my kids, who were genuinely concerned. <:

THE LESSON

Patience comes naturally for Scooby, but for the rest of us it's something we have to work on. Getting angry rarely has any benefits and can cloud your thinking. When people make mistakes, give them a chance to correct the mistakes. Forgive them. Seek the good in people; believe that most people are good. This takes patience. Most good things in life require patience. Delayed gratification is a good thing. As our world continues to become more instantaneous, realize most good things in life are NOT. Instant coffee excluded. Be patient, be kind, be humble, and be loving like Scooby!

CHAPTER 5

LOVE

THROUGHOUT THIS BOOK, you will hear the word *love* used quite a bit, so I thought I might take a moment and share what the word means to me! Let's jump right into "The Lesson."

THE LESSON

We all want to be loved, don't we? Don't you want your spouse or family to love you? How about God? Don't you want him to love you? Say YES, because we are born seeking LOVE. In my opinion, the best way to receive love is, simply, to give it. Give it unconditionally, with no strings attached and no expectations of any benefits you could receive in exchange. Give love without limitations and without expectations. True happiness is most certainly linked to LOVE.

People in your life need to know that you love them. But don't just say it, show them! Surprise them and do something kind they aren't expecting. Call someone you have lost touch with and reconnect. Let your guard down and spread the word. If you are reading this book,

I love you—because I don't expect anyone other than my wife and mom to read it. Love makes me smile, it makes me happy, and the world is a better place because we have it.

If you find yourself grumpy, try doing something nice for someone. Connor, Izzy, Riley, and Jen, I love you guys more than you will ever know! Hopefully, you already know that!

CHAPTER 6

OREO CHEESECAKE

NOW THAT YOU know about Connor, Izzy, Riley, and Scooby, let me tell you about the centerpiece of the Martin family, a person I LOVE very much— Momma Bear Jen Spatz-Martin. Above all else, Jen cares for her family, and every member of our family adores her. She is our selfless caretaker who always puts her family first. She ALWAYS thinks about us first, and we call her Momma Bear because if you mess with any of her cubs, you better look out!

Let me share the story with you about how I met Momma Bear.

It was the fall of 1999 when I met the love of my life, Jennifer Spatz. We were in Columbia, South Carolina, during our final year of college (GO, GAMECOCKS!). I worked at this magical dessert bar named Nonnah's. Nonnah's was owned and managed by Maggie Groff, a transplant from New York. Nonnah's was named after Maggie's daughter Shannon. Spell Nonnah's backward and you will get it. Nonnah's was magical in so many ways. Everyone entered the establishment with great anticipation. All who entered knew they were in for a treat!

I considered myself a pretty cool dude back in 1999. I was one of the primary bartenders at Nonnah's, which made me a bit of a local celebrity. Let me clarify my celebrity status for you: when you are a bartender in a college town, all of your good friends expect to drink for free. Thankfully, Nonnah's wasn't a party bar destination the younger crowd looked to patronize until the early hours of the morning; it was too nice for that. My friends would stop in for a few pregame cocktails, bringing along whatever lady friend they were trying to impress that evening. If you wanted to impress a lady, Nonnah's was the way to go.

The instant you walked through the front door of Nonnah's, your senses were aroused. The distinct smell of coffee and dessert couldn't be avoided; neither could the sound of laughter. Desserts make people happy. The decor perfectly matched the welcoming vibe: the walls were filled with local artwork, and the dessert fridge was the main attraction. Men and women would choose their favorite piece of cake as carefully as they might choose an engagement ring (hint hint). The lighting was perfectly dimmed, leaving just enough of a glow to see the smiles on everyone's faces. South Carolina's state slogan—Smiling Faces, Beautiful Places—aptly described the inside of Nonnah's.

I told you if you wanted to impress a lady you would bring her to Nonnah's. But on one lucky night, Nonnah's brought a lady to me!

Nonnah's consisted of two bars: the main bar with the dessert case and the side bar, which was located in its own room adjacent to the main dining area. On this night, I was working the main bar and a new employee was starting, a new employee that would forever change my world. She was beautiful. She had deep brown eyes and long dark hair. She had my attention right away. I even remember the gray button-down dress she wore that night.

At the University of South Carolina, there were two types of girls: the Southern Belles and the Northerners. The Southern Belles were from the South and were traditionally warm and friendly. On the other side of the coin were the Northerners, who hailed from the Northeast, typically above the Virginia state line. Northerners proudly carried a bit of an edge most of the time. Funny sidenote, if you ask a Northern girl what she thinks of a Southern Belle, she would typically tell you they are fake. If you ask a Southern Belle what she thinks of a Northerner, she would say they are rude.

Their assessments of each other were as equally wrong as they were accurate.

For whatever reason most of the time, the Southern Belles preferred the beaus from the South and the Northerners preferred the fellas from the North. Jennifer Spatz was definitely a Northerner who came with an edge. She was a no-BS girl from Pennsylvania. This Northern girl quickly shared her edgy side with me. Our first conversation sounded something like this.

Jen: Did you work the sidebar last night?
Jason: For sure. Yep, that was me.
Jen: Well, you left it a terrible mess!

That was it. That was how it all got started. That was in September 1999. By Thanksgiving the same year, Jen was coming home with me to meet my parents.

Jen had me at "you left the bar a terrible mess." I was in love quickly; I knew she was the one. We dated four years before I asked her to marry me. I think it took me that long to save up for her ring, not because she required an expensive diamond but rather because I was broke. I cashed out my retirement account (which wasn't much) from the TV station I was working at to buy a ring for her. It was the only savings I had, but she was my girl.

At the time of our engagement, Jen was working for a small startup company in Columbia, South Carolina, and I was the main sports anchor for the FOX station in Wilmington, North Carolina. I would do my final show of the week on Friday night and head straight to Columbia to spend the weekend with my lady. The drive from Wilmington to Columbia takes about three hours, which had me arriving between 1:00 and 2:00 a.m. Oftentimes I struggled to stay awake for the drive, but I missed my girl.

This particular trip, I had a shiny ring burning a hole in my pocket. The previous week, I had called her parents to get their approval. Pop Pop said, "You know she's a pain in the ass, don't you?" He was joking, of course, but his humor put me at ease, and I had permission to proceed.

I had my plan mapped out. Naturally, it had to involve Nonnah's. I had called Maggie, the owner, to share my engagement plan with her. We would go out with a few friends for the evening and then stop in for dessert and a nightcap at Nonnah's. Jen's favorite dessert was Nonnah's famous Oreo cheesecake. I knew that's what she would order.

Maggie was onboard with the plan and agreed to add a question written in chocolate to the perimeter of the plate: WILL YOU MARRY ME? Jen and I were sitting in the front bay window. It was one of the more private, romantic seats. This spot was near the side bar. It was secluded and the main bar wasn't visible from this location (part of the plan). I had shared my plan with all of our friends, who were secretly gathering on the other side of the restaurant at the main bar.

Soon, it was time for dessert—and time to pop the question. I don't think Jen had any clue about my plan. Maggie delivered the cake, and I got down on one knee. It was a very special moment, and so was the surprise engagement party I had waiting for us on the other side of the restaurant. We walked over to the main bar where our friends were anxiously awaiting our arrival. We were greeted with smiles, cheers, and the popping sounds of champagne corks.

In September 2003, Jen and I got married on the horseshoe of the University of South Carolina. She looked amazing on our wedding day. Now, three kids and a dog later, that moment seems so long ago, but the memory is as crisp as a fall day.

THE LESSON

You never know when love will find you. Marriage is sacred and takes work. You should never take it for granted. Everything in life that's important to you will take work, will need attention. Make sure your marriage is a priority. Make sure the person you marry matches up with your core values. When you marry someone, remember you are also marrying into their family. Make sure you not only love your spouse but that you love their family as well. I love Pop Pop's jokes and Mom Mom always lets me beat her at Zilch. (Zilch is a dice game the family plays together during the holidays. For the record, I am the Zilch champion.)

The person you are marrying comes as a package with their family. Even though I fell in love with Jen instantly, it was important to make sure we were in the right place in our lives to memorialize our lifelong commitment to each other. Don't rush into marriage. Take your time, and make sure it's the person you want to spend the rest of your life with. Even then, you will make many mistakes in your marriage. Be humble, be loving, be forgiving, and eat Oreo cheesecake. Honey, I love you!

CHAPTER 7

AND NOW BATTING

YOUR DAD IS a dreamer, and I want you to be a dreamer too!

I am a believer in the power of dreams. Dreaming is something my mom instilled in me at a very young age. She always made sure I knew I could be whoever I wanted to be in life and that it was up to me. She never questioned my dreams; she simply said, "Go for it! You can do it!"

I dreamed of one day becoming a sports anchor. My favorite sound was the sound of my own voice. I didn't need an audience, just a mic and my Fender guitar amp. One of my favorite things to do as a child was to call a game. I transformed our living room into my own broadcast booth. I would turn on the Baltimore Orioles, mute the volume, and begin doing play-by-play announcing. "And now batting for the Baltimore Orioles: Cal Ripken Jr.!" It's no surprise that in my high school yearbook I said my life goal was to become a sports anchor, and that's exactly what I did. I accomplished my childhood dream and pursued my passion.

I wanted to put my vision into action at a very young age, so I didn't just let my dream float around in my brain. I aggressively pursued it. I was the sports editor of my high school newspaper, the public address announcer for women's basketball and JV football, and, by the time my senior year arrived, I was getting paid to cover sports for the local county paper. I can't remember the exact amount I was getting paid. Let's just say it might have covered a tank of gas, but it was a big deal to me regardless.

If I had the opportunity to do something related to my dream, that's what I did. I even turned my high school "history" project into a recorded sports show. The project was called Athletes, Fans, and the Media. I am not sure how athletes, fans, and the media related to history, but somehow my friend Greg and I pulled it off.

Our guests on the show included Chris Hamburger, a retired Washington Redskin, and Ken Mease, the local sports anchor from the CBS affiliate. I told you, if I could find a way to tie in my dream to a project, that's what I did. Ken Mease invited us to the station to do the interview and I was pumped. He was kind enough to give us a tour of the studio, which only confirmed what I already knew: I was going to become a sports anchor. Walking through the studio was equivalent to a child getting a tour of the North Pole. While Ken wasn't Santa Claus,

I did make sure to share my dream with him that day, and he invited me to stay in touch, something I took full advantage of. That connection with Ken landed me an internship at the station my sophomore year of college. WUSA Channel 9 was the top station in a major market: Washington, DC. **Lesson #1: Share your dreams.**

Dreaming is addictive, and I have discovered that rarely do dreamers only have one dream. We have many. I not only dreamed of becoming a sports anchor; I also dreamed of attending the University of South Carolina. When a big envelope arrived in the mail that said "accepted student" on the outside, I was on the moon. The University of South Carolina had an excellent broadcast program that included a television studio where shows were recorded daily. South Carolina's broadcast department was a talent pool for local area stations. Several times each semester, news directors from local stations would stop in and check out the show, check out the talent. As a point of reference, news directors were often in charge of hiring. If a news director showed up for the recording of a show, you wanted to be sharp. It felt just like an audition regardless of whether the station was currently hiring.

By senior year, I was the University's sports anchor. During one of our tapings, the news director from the local station in Augusta, Georgia, stopped in. She gave

me her card and told me to call her just before I gradu-
ated. I was pumped! Of course, I called her and my first
job out of college was working for WJBF, an ABC affiliate. **Lesson #2: Make connections.**

I was not hired as the sports anchor for WJBF, but
as a news videographer, better described as the cam-
eraman. The news director who hired me understood
my goal was to become a sports anchor and promised
me that she would eventually work me into the sports
department. I understood there weren't any openings in
the sports department (yet). This was a starting point
and I needed experience. I spent forty hours a week covering news as a videographer. After my paid workday
was complete with the news department, I devoted my
time helping out the sports department (for free) with
anything they needed.

A few months later, my childhood dream became
reality. I was ON-AIR for the first time covering high
school football. In Georgia, high school football is a
big deal and my first spot was covering a game for the
show "Football Friday Night." To say I was nervous is
an understatement. My entire life I wanted to be a sports
anchor and it was time to go live! My first on-air spot
lasted about thirty seconds. I am certain I sounded like
a twelve-year-old boy going through puberty that night,
not a seasoned professional, but it didn't matter. My

dream just became reality. I eventually worked my way up at WJBF as the fill-in sports anchor. **Lesson #3: Pay your dues.**

The main sports anchor and the weekend anchor at WJBF station didn't appear to be giving up their seats on the anchor desk any time soon, so I needed a solution. I needed to find a station where I would be the main anchor—or at least the weekend guy. I noticed a job opening in Wilmington, North Carolina, for the main sports anchor slot. I quickly called the station's news director to ask if I could drop off my résumé tape in person. He obliged, and I made the 280-mile trip there (one-way).

When I arrived, I noticed a *very* large pile of résumé tapes on his desk. Lots of tapes that never got reviewed. A few days later, I got the call I was going to be the number-one guy for WSFX in Wilmington, North Carolina. The news director appreciated the extra effort I made to drop off the tape. If I had just mailed in my résumé tape like everyone else, this story would look entirely different. I was living the dream! It's a pretty cool thing to the be the number-one sports anchor at the young age of twenty-three. **Lesson #4: When you see an opportunity, don't wait! Get in your car!**

My days in sports broadcasting are memories that I will keep forever. I got to meet Michael Jordan, Hank Aaron, and Arnold Palmer and cover the Masters! You might be asking yourself, why I am no longer chasing that dream? My goals in life changed. I wanted to get married, have children, and start making a little more money. I don't regret chasing my dream at all. I get to say for the rest of my life I did it! I have new dreams today that I am chasing. I hope I never stop dreaming. If you really want to have a chance to experience your dream in life, it requires action, which leads me to my final lesson of this chapter. **Lesson #5: Dreams without action are just dreams.**

THE LESSONS

#1: Share your dreams.

#2: Make connections.

#3: Pay your dues.

#4: When you see opportunity, don't wait.

#5: Dreams without actions are just dreams.

CHAPTER 8

THIS BOOK

SINCE WE ARE talking about dreams, let me share one of my most recent dreams with you. I told you dreamers never have just one dream. This book is a dream.

Five years in the making, and my first draft was complete—dream complete. I was an author; the hard work was over. A few rounds of editing, and it would be time for my book release party. I could visualize the location and who would be in attendance. I even began practicing what I was going to say. "It's so exciting to see all of my family and friends here today. I want you to know that wherever you are in your life today, *you* can keep growing, you can do things you never thought possible, regardless of your age. I never thought I would be an author or be speaking at my own book release party, but here I am, and I am so grateful you are here to share the experience with me." Exciting, right?

Then it was time to hand off my first draft to the editor. I expected a few tweaks and on to publishing. I started visualizing what the cover would like, the size, the font, the foreword, and all the fun details that accompany completion. I was way ahead of myself!

When I was a student at the University of South Carolina, the most difficult course in my curriculum was copyediting with Dr. Henry Price. I just got chills thinking about the course while writing this chapter; I conveniently forgot how terrible I am at editing anything, much less my own book. At least 50 percent of Dr. Price's students failed the course on their first go-round. No surprise here, I failed at first too. Thankfully I received a passing score of C+ on my second attempt. Copyediting was a required course for journalism majors, and you weren't allowed to proceed without passing the course. I now realize that copy editing with Dr. Price actually prepared me for what was about to happen with my own book.

My editor sent me an email a few days prior to our first draft review call. She wanted to know what message I wanted to convey in the book, who was my avatar, who is the book for? I couldn't wait for our Zoom call. I was certain I had created a New York Times best seller. Do you remember the movie *A Christmas Story*, where Ralphie hands in his Christmas-themed paper? Ralphie was a second-grader who wanted a Red Ryder BB gun for Christmas and the chosen topic for the paper was something he was passionate about: "What I Want for Christmas." Ralphie was pumped. As he handed in his paper, the camera shared the thoughts bouncing around inside Ralphie's head. He had created a masterpiece. He daydreamed about the rave reviews his paper was sure to receive. Ralphie was going to get an A++++. He was devastated when his teacher Miss Shields gave him a C+. Turns out, I was just like Ralphie, except I didn't even get a C+ on my first review. The editor said, "Go back to the drawing board. I think you missed your mark." Dagger!

It legitimately crushed my soul. My book release party would have to wait. My editor punched me in the gut, took my breath away. I poured my heart and soul into my first draft. To say I was crushed was an understatement. I stopped writing for three weeks. It took my pride that long to recover.

My writing journey began about five years ago while I was having lunch with a friend who had recently released her first book. I was curious about what she thought of her experience. I think it's exciting when people do things they have never done before. She basically told me you have to lock yourself in a room and write for hours each day. You need to build your writing muscle. Writing didn't sound fun or exciting to me; it sounded like torture. I admired people who could do it, but nothing about locking myself in a room writing for several hours each day appealed to me at all.

One year later, I found myself in the office of best-selling author Pastor Mark Batterson with my daughter

Izzy. Izzy loves reading books, so I have encouraged her to write her own book one day. I wanted to teach Izzy about the benefits of asking questions of those who have done what you would like to do. Asking questions is a skill set and a powerful tool to have in your arsenal. It's so important that we will talk more about questions in a few chapters. Pastor Mark was kind enough to answer all of our questions, sharing his writing secrets. We learned that when it's writing season for Pastor Mark, he lets very few things make it on to his schedule. In other words, writing is a priority and takes daily practice. By the way, Izzy, I still expect you to be an author one day!

A few months after that meeting, my brain decided that writing a book was something I could do! I shared the idea with Izzy that I wanted to write a book. I wanted to show her Dad could do it, and I began racking my brain to come up with the title. (If you are considering writing a book, I suggest writing the book before worrying about the title.) I reserved my domain name (howandwhynotme.com) and I was convinced this was going to work. The book was going to be about doing things you didn't know you could do: how and why not me? I had it all mapped out before writing my first word! A few years later, not a single chapter was drafted . . . but at least I had the title and domain name locked in. Unfortunately, I was answering my own question of "Why not me," because I had yet to write a single word.

Howandwhynotme.com started to sound more like Not Me because I didn't seem to be moving toward the starting line, let alone the finish line. But thankfully after a few Go Daddy renewal cycles, I got tired of hearing myself talk about writing a book and decided it was time to proceed. I finally decided to go ALL IN. Five short years after my brain began exploring the idea of writing, I issued a personal challenge to myself.

Once I committed, I hired a coach. I knew I needed direction and accountability. This book wouldn't have happened without the help of my coach and friend Azul Terronez, who ever so patiently helped me get this book finished. As an added layer of self-accountability, I told all my friends and family members I was going to become an author well before the first chapter was written. I fully understood that once I shared my dream with family and friends, there would be no turning back. Telling them I couldn't finish what I started just isn't in my DNA. I knew these accountability steps were necessary. Sometimes in life you have to do things to make sure your mind has little wriggle room to escape. I do believe you can train/trick your brain into the direction you want to go.

THE LESSON

You have to challenge yourself in life. Writing a book was a huge challenge for me. Writing has never been my strong suit and likely still isn't. <; I have learned so much while writing this book, though. I have stretched myself and allowed my brain to explore new adventures. I don't regret a single minute of the decision, even if it took me five years from start to finish.

Issue yourself a personal challenge even if you have doubts. Go ALL IN on completing the challenge. You will never know how high you can climb unless you test the boundaries of your preconceived limits. Challenge yourself and—who knows—you might get to call yourself an author one day! It's fun when your previous ceiling becomes your new floor. This doesn't happen if you don't challenge yourself.

CHAPTER 9

GET BACK
ON THE ICE

WHEN YOU ARE a dreamer and challenge your-self, good things are going to happen in your life. As you learned in the last chapter, you also have to learn how to recover from failure. Here's a hint: it's only called failure if you don't get back up once you are knocked down.

Let's talk about the F-word for a few minutes. I am not talking about the one that rhymes with PUCK . . . I am talking about Failure. Failure is that feeling of defeat, that punch in the gut that takes your breath away. Failure makes me want to say the word that rhymes with PUCK. Failure is also a wonderful opportunity: an opportunity to reinvent yourself. It's a rite of passage, and it's often a precursor to success.

I remember when my son, Connor, first decided to play hockey. He was so excited the night before his first practice, he barely got any sleep. Hockey was the only thing on his mind. We were geared up and ready. The National Hockey League was waiting. Geared up means we purchased the equipment required to play: helmet, stick, gloves, shoulder pads, pants, etc. The only thing we didn't have to purchase was skates because a neighbor generously donated an old pair that no longer fit his son. I was happy that I didn't have to add the cost of new skates to my expensive equipment tab (yet). But even with the donation, it was almost a thousand dollars later that we were ready to begin his NHL journey.

A few minutes into his very first practice, instead of skating toward the net for a goal, he was headed for the exit. As he skated to the rink exit, I knew something wasn't right. His eyes filled with water. His tiny legs, feet, and ankles were in pain making it difficult for him to skate. I love my son more than anything in the world and I knew how badly he desired to play hockey. His feet and ankles weren't the only thing hurting; his pride was bruised.

My heart was broken. Just minutes into his first practice, his dreams were shattered. If I hadn't been surrounded by lots of hockey parents, I would have cried with him. I could relate to the emotional pain he was feeling. Sure, his feet hurt, but what really hurt was his pride. It's that feeling of defeat, that feeling of failure.

This couldn't be the end of his career. The Martins don't give up that easily. I needed to think fast. I knew I had to get him back on the ice. I needed an out, a way to recapture Connor's excitement. This wasn't the right time for me to give him a pep talk. I had to be more strategic than that. Clearly it was the old skates causing the problems (wink, wink). The next day we purchased a brand-new pair of skates. Connor still didn't want to play, but the new skates offered just enough hope for Connor to try again. Funny enough, I learned during his new skate fitting that his old skates were actually a size and a half too small. Maybe it *was* the skates!

We were back on the ice. I promised Connor he could come off the ice any time with no questions asked if he just gave it one more chance. This was a big gamble on my part. Any hockey player will tell you the first time you use a new pair of skates your feet absolutely hurt. It takes a few practices to break the skates in. This made it very likely that he would once again have sore feet and ankles. I knew I wasn't going to get a third chance with Connor. As he stepped on the ice for his second practice, I watched anxiously, praying my plan would work. This time Connor once again skated for the exit, not because he wanted to leave the ice but because practice was over! This time when he looked up at me, instead of tears he had a tiny smile. That was all I needed to see. Victory was ours!

Three years ago, he wanted to quit. Now he lives for hockey. He is what I call a hockey junkie. He constantly wants to be on the ice. If he's not on the ice, he's playing street hockey or taping new sticks. It's hockey 24/7 for my main man.

I am proud of my son in so many ways. His first season on the ice wasn't exactly a season filled with goals; in fact, he didn't score a single goal his first season. . . . Season two Connor led his team in assists and was second in goals scored. When Connor scored his first career goal, it was such an exciting moment for both of us. Connor kept that puck. I love that puck! It's not about the goals; it's about getting back on the ice even when your feet hurt.

THE LESSON

After forty-three trips around the sun, I have learned how to deal with the F-word: failure. I didn't say I like failure, but I have learned how to deal with it. It's not easy dealing with failure, especially if you put in the effort and fail anyway. Effort doesn't always equal the results you think you should get. Many times in my life, I have been disappointed.

Failure only means failure if you decide to let it. Sometimes you just need to change course a bit. A famous boxer from my day, Mike Tyson, described it well: "Everyone has a plan until you get punched in the face." Life is going to punch you in the face. When it happens, it definitely hurts. When life punches you in the face, just do what Connor did. Get back on the ice!

CHAPTER 10

2 GOLDS, 1 SILVER

A FEW YEARS BACK, my twins decided they wanted to do kempo (a.k.a., karate). Kempo has a variety of forms, but the Martins favor sparring above all else. Sparring involves direct contact with your opponent through kicks or punches, and you can get hurt. Before you get too worried, kicks are only allowed above the waist and each student is required to wear gloves and protective headgear. Connor and Izzy craved the contact. They enjoyed delivering punches or landing a few sidekicks. My twins are competitive (primarily with each other), and sparring seemed to come naturally. I believe Connor and Izzy inherited this trait from me as I welcome competition. I often remind my family that Dad is an athlete. <;

Each week, I would head to the karate dojo to watch my kids train. Typically, at the end of each class, the students get to spar with each other. The instructor picks two students, puts them in a ring, and yells, "Fight!" Imagine a scaled-down version of the movie *Karate Kid*! The first student to successfully land three points is the victor. When you are in the ring and the instructor yells,

"Fight," your heart rate doubles. Sparring is not for everyone, but, like I mentioned, it happens to be the Martins' preferred event.

Every week, I anxiously watched my kids' sparring matches, hoping they would land the first punch! I wasn't the only parent watching with enthusiasm—everyone wants their kid to win—but the instructor could tell that sparring piqued my curiosity. One evening as the kids' class was wrapping up, he let me know that he also runs an adult class and thought I should give it a shot. I couldn't resist. I had dabbled in karate a few times throughout my life, so I wasn't a total newbie.

For the adults, Friday night was fight night: nonstop sparring for an hour. I absolutely loved it. Sparring is an incredible full-body workout. It was the perfect way to end a week. In about three minutes, I would sweat away whatever stresses were on my mind. My entire gee (karate uniform) would be drenched in sweat and I loved it. Sparring on Friday night usually required a long, Epsom-soaked bath and two Advil liquid gel caps afterward to help relieve the pain I just caused myself. I was usually a little stiff on Saturday morning, with plenty of battle scars to show from the previous night's work. My wife nicknamed Friday night sparring "old man sparring."

Old man sparring is fun for me but even more fun are the semiannual tournaments. The most exciting time of the year for karate students are the tournaments, where you get a chance to truly test your skills. The tournaments were always packed with students, parents, and grandparents, creating a standing-room-only setting. The most watched/anticipated event is always sparring.

On this day, somehow, someway, I had made it to the championship match. My entire family was watching. I was nervous for certain, but I had no intentions of letting my nerves show. I believed I was better than all of my previous opponents, but my opponent in the championship match was a master craftsman. His hands were weapons, and his kicks were powerful. With one swift kick to my head, I knew my opponent could end my day—if not my sparring career. I was about to get my ass kicked. I had witnessed my opponent obliterate people all day.

I tried not to let my nerves show with my family looking on, but make no mistake, I was scared. I decided to have a quick pep talk with myself that went something like this: "You're probably going to get your ass kicked, but you made it this far. Why not go all in? Just go for it!" We entered the ring and the instructor yelled, "Fight!" I decided prior to the match that the only way I was going to win was to strike first. I knew that if I sat back and waited, I would get shredded. As soon as the fight started, my heart beating through my chest, I jumped in the air and landed my first point: a hammer strike to the head.

The first participant to earn three points wins, and I was up 1-0. Point two I landed a sidekick to his rib cage. I was up 2-0, but the match was far from over. My opponent battled back with a few tricks of his own and tied the score 2-2. The next point wins the gold! I could hear my daughter cheering in the background, "Come on, Dad, you got this!" At that moment, I reminded myself again, "You might as well go ALL IN. You made it this far." I attacked and landed a front kick. Dad won!

This was a very special day. Izzy won the gold in sparring, Connor won the silver in sparring, and Dad won the gold. I actually think my son should have won the gold as well, but the judges missed a point. Connor, Izzy, and I were floating on cloud nine. You would have thought we just won Olympic medals. For many weeks after the tournament, my wife got the great honor of hearing about how she was living in a house of champions.

THE LESSON

Sometimes in life you have to go all in. You might lose, but you might not. It's unlikely you will win if you don't go all in. When it comes to your career, pick a path and go all in. You might change careers a few times in your life and that's okay, but go all in with every decision so you know what that feels like. It's a good thing. Life changes and you will also, but at least you know how to give something your all. You don't win the gold if you don't go all in.

A quick sidenote, during the tournament I was an orange belt. An orange belt is just a few belts above a beginner. I bet you thought I was a black belt by the way I told the story! In my mind on that day, I was a black belt, and I went all in.

The Champions

CHAPTER 11

THE RED LEAF

M Y FAMILY GOES all in on birthdays. Every year in the late summer, I jog along the George Washington Parkway looking for the perfect birthday leaf. It's a beautiful trail on the Potomac River that leads to the former home of George and Martha Washington. Something about the trail inspires me. I can't quite put my finger on it, but some of my best thoughts happen when I am jogging or riding my bike on that trail. It gives me hope and inspiration.

The trail becomes truly inspirational late in the summer when the trees start changing colors. The air becomes crisp and the color combinations are beyond beautiful. Green leaves turn vibrant red, orange, and yellow. Usually the first color to appear is red. During this special time of year, at the end of a long run I grab the biggest brightest red leaf I can find. I gently carry the treasure home with me.

Full of energy and life, I share my treasure with my kids. They know what happens next. I let them know that the red leaf indicates that fall is coming, which means their birthdays will soon be arriving. All three of our children were born in the fall, and by the time I present them with my treasure, their birthday wish lists have long been established and proudly displayed on our refrigerator. In our house, my kids begin making plans for the next birthday immediately after their previous one ends.

To me, the leaf is more than a leaf. It's symbolic of how much I love my children. It reminds them that I am thinking about them, that I want to share in their excitement, and that their special day is very special to me. They use the presentation of the leaf as an opportunity to remind me of what's on their wish list. In fact, they take full advantage of the situation, usually adding a few additional items. I can't remember everything on their list, but somehow Momma Bear never forgets a single thing.

Each year, their birthday plans seemingly get bigger. I love their enthusiasm because it means my kids are dreamers; they have hope. I never want any of my family members to stop hoping, to stop dreaming. Sometimes we have to scale down their expectations, but I genuinely love their excitement. As a dreamer, I always like having things to hope for, things to look forward to. Hope gives me energy; hope breathes life into my lungs! I am excited just writing about it.

We have things to look forward to year-round. Some of the things we hope for require years of planning, like a family trip to Australia or Hawaii (maybe both <;). We look forward to Thanksgiving, Christmas, summer boat rides, Maryland blue crabs, beach trips, ice cream! When one box is checked, we often begin fantasizing about the next.

We are the family who puts the Christmas tree up on Thanksgiving weekend, and if you visit us in February, the tree will be waiting. By December 10, we have watched all of our favorite holiday movies. Our favorites include *Elf* and *The Grinch*, but *Christmas Vacation* is quickly climbing to the top as my children currently find curse words very funny. Their favorite part of the movie is when Chevy Chase tells his corporate coworkers to kiss his ass! It is quite funny. I prefer the classics like *Rudolph*, but I have to fight to get that one in rotation.

We get excited about so many things like pumpkin chocolate dessert bread. We call it crack bread—I know, not a good name, but truth be told you have less than twenty-four hours to grab a slice. Generally, we are a kind, sharing family. But when it comes to the crack bread, sharing isn't part of the equation. We purchase it from the local farmers market, so the bread is only available certain times of year. Once it's in our house, it's gone fast. We even lick the crumbs from our plates.

THE LESSON

My entire point about hope is this: never stop hoping; never stop dreaming. Hope doesn't always have to consist of grand ideas. It can be as simple as hoping for the first snowfall of the season so you can go sledding. Just to be clear, flushing an ice cube down the toilet doesn't really work! Whoever created that game, anyway? Hope can be as simple as hoping to see a full moon or getting excited about a sunrise.

I hope that for your entire life, hope is always a part of the equation. I hope that I will always give you a red leaf on your birthday. Keep hope with you at all times, regardless of what season of life you are in.

CHAPTER 12

PMA

W HEN I WAS in sixth grade, I was lucky enough to have a teacher, Morris Hawkins, who forever changed my world. Morris Hawkins was a cool cat in his early sixties. He always wore a sport coat and tie, but he wasn't a stiff. He sported a white goatee and resembled KFC's Colonel Saunders. Mr. Hawkins wasn't an intimidator, but he was definitely someone you wanted to respect you. He was that teacher you didn't want to disappoint. Morris Hawkins was cool; in fact, he was more the just cool. He was calm, encouraging, and optimistic, and he understood how to connect with sixth-graders.

Our middle school was crowded, creating the need for additional classrooms. Morris Hawkins's classroom was located in a trailer just outside the main campus. Classes inside of trailers were typically loud and rambunctious, as the four walls acted like sound springboards. Trailer classes typically created a more chaotic atmosphere than those inside the main campus; however, chaos did not exist in Morris Hawkins's classroom. The rhythm of his class matched the tone of his personality. Mr. Hawkins had a special gift that allowed him to retain a sixth-grader's attention—not an easy task. In sixth grade, energy is bubbling, emotions run high, and puberty is beginning to take hold. Keeping a rambunctious group of sixth-graders calm is an almost impossible task, but Morris Hawkins did it with ease. When he spoke, we listened.

One fall day back in 1988, three simple letters changed my life. As we gathered in the classroom, three very big letters were written on the board. We took our seats and wondered what we were in for. What did PMA mean? These letters were written in oversized font on the chalkboard in front of the room. They were impossible to ignore. Mr. Hawkins had our attention before saying a single word. We settled in quickly and the classroom became completely silent as we anxiously awaited the words of wisdom that were about to be shared with us.

In his calming yet attention-demanding voice, Morris Hawkins proclaimed that PMA stands for Positive Mental Attitude. He decided to spend the entire day's lesson on these three simple letters that I will keep with me until the day I die. There is so much I love about the lesson. One day, three letters, and words of wisdom that I hope to pass on to anyone who will listen. If you are a teacher reading this, notice how we weren't talking about details, facts, or equations. Morris Hawkins was teaching us how to think. More than any other lesson during *all* of my years of education, including college, this simple lesson is the one I found the most valuable. PMA is something I always strive for. Like anything good in life, though, it takes work.

I often wonder if the lesson had the same impact on the other students in the classroom that day. When I am struggling to stay positive, I fall back on PMA. I focus on PMA, and I remind myself that I have two options. I can have a positive mental attitude or I can choose not to. I don't care if you are the happiest person in the world, I promise you will find yourself in a slump. It's easy to have a negative mental attitude when life isn't going your way. Does having a negative attitude *ever* make things better? You already know the answer.

Every spring break we pack up the family minivan and head out on a fun family adventure. We usually go sun chasing to break up the long, cold Northeast winters. This particular spring break, we were headed to South Carolina, and it was anything but fun.

The plan was to meet up with Grandma and Grandad and the cousins at the family home in Surfside Beach. In late March/early April, South Carolina typically provides some warm sunshine, exactly what we need after a chilly winter.

One of my favorite parts of any family trip is when the captain (that's me) pretends to get on the microphone. It usually goes something like this: "This is your captain speaking. We are en route to Surfside Beach, where the weather is 75 degrees and sunny. Travel time today is about eight hours, and if you need anything at all, the fine young lady sitting next to me (that's Mom) will be happy to help." Inevitably, within three minutes of departure, Jen is out of her seat grabbing something the kids need!

We look forward to spring break the entire year! However, this year our enthusiasm quickly turned to concern as the check engine light on the minivan began blinking. With a family of five and a dog, stops are certainly expected, but stopping at the auto dealer to find out what's wrong with the mini wasn't part of the plan. Jen and I wrestled with the idea of ignoring the warning light, but we had way too many miles ahead of us to just ignore it, so we located a dealership and pulled in for what we hoped would be a quick pit stop. We patiently sat in the waiting room for two hours while the car was being repaired. We also included our then-four-month-old puppy Scooby, who thankfully provided some entertainment. We created a makeshift playpen so he wouldn't be able to escape. I think he peed a little on the rug, and his piercing puppy bark had the entire dealership giving us strange looks.

After two long hours, our car was ready and we were back on the road. Good times are waiting (so we thought). Ninety miles after our two-hour delay, the check engine light came on again. This time we certainly would have ignored it, but our car was now making funny noises and having trouble accelerating.

I can't make this up. We pulled off the next exit and literally coasted into the next auto dealer. The car crept into the parking lot and died! That was its own miracle, because we could have just as easily been stuck on the side of I-95 South.

It was now around 5:00 p.m., and the dealer was about to close for the evening, which meant we would have to leave the car overnight. We pivoted. We could just grab a hotel room. Wait, that won't work. We had Scooby, and I am *highly* allergic to most animals, so staying in a pet-friendly hotel room would have been a problem. Plan B: let's get a rental car for the week and just pick the mini up on the way home. Great idea, if we weren't in a small southern town in North Carolina where all three rental car facilities close at 5:00 (it was 5:15). I called anyway, hoping someone would pick up. Thankfully, one of the managers who was locking up for the evening answered (miracle #2). He felt bad for me after I shared my story and promised he would wait until we arrived.

We were back on the road again. The Griswolds—a.k.a., the Martins—weren't going to be denied. Jen and I laughed quite a bit at that family comparison. I guess that's what makes the National Lampoon movie series so good. For families, the humor is all too relatable. Late in the evening, we finally arrived. Normally an eight-hour trip, on this day it took us at least thirteen. The trip was off to a rough start, but we were staying positive.

The next morning after our exhausting day of travel, our daughter Izzy came down with the stomach flu. Not just any flu, either. This was the highly contagious variety that involved three days of vomiting and fever. My wife is a warrior when the kids get sick, but as you can imagine, she became the next victim, followed by Scooby the dog, who decided to vomit on me!

This trip was becoming a disaster. I had to dig deep to find my PMA. At least Connor and Riley were healthy. They were excited and ready for a good time, anxiously awaiting the arrival of the cousins. But it turns out our niece Emily was scheduled to have her tonsils taken out the following week, so they decided it wasn't worth the risk to get her sick. No cousins after all. Now Connor and Riley were heartbroken, Izzy was sick, Jen was sick, our car was in the shop, and Scooby vomited on me.

The entire family was mentally and physically exhausted. At least we were in sunny, warm South Carolina. Except this week it WASN'T sunny. A cold front had moved in. No warm breezes hit us until the last day. Just in time for our departure. I have never been so excited to return home from a trip.

This trip presented us with only two options: a negative mental attitude or a positive mental attitude. Jen and I chose PMA and laughed so hard on the ride home that our stomachs hurt. Admittedly, so did our wallets, as the minivan repairs were in thousands, and that didn't include the weekly car rental.

THE LESSON

I don't know how we did it, but we kept a positive mental attitude. When things aren't going your way, keeping a positive mental attitude will help you get through. It can take effort, believe me. The good news is that it provided some material for this book. PMA— it's always a better way even when life throws you a curveball. Positive mental attitude is a mindset that can change your world. It has mine. You can't always control the things that happen to you in life. However, you *can* control how you react and how you move forward. PMA is *always* available to you in every situation if you choose to use it.

CHAPTER 13

HAPPINESS

A T THE END of the day, PMA is a mindset I hope you choose to incorporate into your life. Choosing to do so will help lead you to a sacred place in your heart: happiness. I so desperately want you guys to be happy.

When it comes to happiness, I hope you seek it, study it, document it, understand it, and live it. Life is precious and life is short. I am the best version of myself when I am happy. It's a state of mind; it's living in the moment. Happiness is visible. You can see joy in a person's eyes and hear it in their voices. But, much like the pursuit of anything in your life worth fighting for, happiness takes work.

Hap·pi·ness, noun—the state of being happy. For most children, happiness comes naturally. Happiness is using their imagination; happiness is playing. It's not forced; it's just fun. As we get older, the world tries to define happiness for us. Reject it! Reject the world's definition of happiness and create your own. Remember when you were a kid, you loved playing. It was fun; you were happy! It was simple, it was pure, and you were in the moment.

As an adult, happiness may not come as naturally as it did when you were a child, but you can find that joy again. You must be thoughtful about seeking happiness, but you should absolutely pursue it. I promise you, *you* are the best version of yourself when you are happy. Don't mistake what I am saying here. You won't always be happy, as life is going to happen and it doesn't always work out the way you think it should. When you are not happy, correct course.

Happiness is a journey, not a destination. The journey is all about you. Be the best version of yourself you can be and happiness will surely be located. Don't worry about what others will think of your journey. It's your journey, not theirs. When you are the best version of yourself possible, those who matter most to you will reap the benefits. That's happiness.

Happiness is when you get lost in the moment. Happiness, to me, is being a dad. Over the years I have tried to capture happiness by writing about it in my journal. Here are some of my favorite moments:

JOURNAL ENTRY JANUARY 6, 2014

The great thing about life at the moment is that I have everything I need: a great family and a warm home.

JOURNAL ENTRY JANUARY 26, 2014

Connor left a little ninja on my work desk. The kids frequently leave me little surprises. I am sure they don't think I notice, but I do. Every so often your life comes into harmony. I mean spiritual, marriage, kids, professional. I am headed into one of those grooves, and it's helping me grow as a person.

JOURNAL ENTRY APRIL 27, 2014

Today was 72 degrees, and we enjoyed every minute of it. Jen and the kids decided to plant a garden today in the backyard. They planted all sorts of fruit and vegetable seeds.

JOURNAL ENTRY OCTOBER 14, 2014

I just can't be any happier. I often wonder what took me so long to find this perfect spot in life. I want to see how long I can stay in the groove.

JOURNAL ENTRY APRIL 22, 2015

I took the twins to the bus stop this morning, and I am encouraged to say that at this point we all still yell LOVE YOU to each other before they get on the bus. This won't last forever, but it's still cool to me.

JOURNAL ENTRY JULY 4, 2015

This week we visited Mountain Lake Lodge in Blacksburg, Virginia. No TVs, just natural fun. We went on two hikes. The first day our hike was through what felt like a jungle (seriously). The second day we hiked to Cascade Falls. The hike was four miles in total over lots of slippery rocks. At the top was a sixty-six-foot waterfall. It was an amazing and beautiful day.

Cascade Falls, Giles County, Virginia

Sometimes to find happiness you need to unplug from the world. Sometimes you have to go chasing waterfalls!

JOURNAL ENTRY NOVEMBER 6, 2015

Our neighborhood is in full color, what a special time of year. Halloween was great. We were the Ghostbusters.

JOURNAL ENTRY DECEMBER 9, 2016

Connor captured a lizard which he has decided to keep on our front porch. He has managed to keep it alive for two months. Last night we purchased crickets from PetCo in case the lizard gets hungry.

JOURNAL ENTRY MAY 12, 2017

Riley lost her first tooth and rides her bike all around the block with no training wheels. Connor had a good week. He caught two chipmunks, one field mouse, one lizard, and one bird. Izzy is getting so tall and she reads books all the time.

JOURNAL ENTRY AUGUST 12, 2017

Where to start with this one. The family vacation started nine days ago; we are having a blast. It started in San Fran where we took an old fire engine ride across the Golden Gate Bridge. We stopped in the Buena Vista Cafe for some Irish coffee and of course we made the trip to Full/ Fuller House.

Connor, Riley, Izzy, and Dad

From San Fran, we made our way to Berkley where we stayed at the very fancy Claremont Hotel. Our night was perfect as we watched the sun set in the lobby while listening to live music followed by a game of OLD MAID with the kids.

JOURNAL ENTRY MAY 7, 2018

I had a great day yesterday. Riley and I walked over to the playground, then took a short hike on the trail. Connor and I played street hockey, Izzy and I played soccer, then I played a game of old man basketball with the neighbors. I just really appreciated the day.

What made the day so great is that I was living in the moment, spending time with the people who matter most to me. Happiness should not be complicated. It should be simple, and you should make it a daily priority. All of my favorite days in life have been when I am living in the moment. Some of your best memories of your own life will be when you are in the moment too.

JOURNAL ENTRY APRIL 12, 2019

We just returned from spring break in Cozumel, Mexico. Our favorite day was at Paradise Beach, which included snorkeling with lots of colorful fish. We couldn't figure out if the barracuda wanted to be our friend or not.

JOURNAL ENTRY JULY 10, 2020

I believe my family can reach for the stars and maybe even touch them. With the help of the Lord, we have no limits!

I have many more journal entries just like these. A strange phenomenon happens when I review my past entries of moments that made me happy. My brain remembers how happy I was during the moment and instantly makes me happy again! I get the joy of reliving the memory every time I read it.

THE LESSON

I am going to make this short so you will not forget it. Life is short. Be *happy*, even during a global pandemic.

CHAPTER 14

COVID-19

WHEN COVID-19 HIT the world in 2020, we weren't quite sure what would happen. The first two or three weeks were surrounded by confusion, disbelief, and a hope that a cure would quickly surface. In the spring of 2020, one by one states began closing down. Restaurants, bars, retail shops, and basically all nonessential businesses shut their doors. Even schools were shut down!

The global pandemic that killed hundreds of thousands worldwide is like nothing I have witnessed in my lifetime. The fear of the unknown is terrifying. A majority of the top health officials are warning that those with preexisting medical conditions have the highest risk of death. That would be me. I have had asthma since I was born. On many occasions, I can remember trips to the emergency room because I couldn't breathe. I am certain asthma almost killed me on more than one occasion. When I was growing up doctors didn't recommend rescue inhalers for children. That basically meant if I had an asthma attack, I didn't have an instant remedy in my pocket. No life jacket, so to speak. If I had an attack, it was off to the emergency room.

If you know anything about asthma attacks, it's not like a cold that runs its course. Your lungs lose capacity to take in oxygen; your breaths become shorter and shorter. Just imagine what a fish might feel like when they are out of water. Considering my multiple near-death experiences with asthma, you might think contracting COVID-19 as a "high-risk" individual would be weighing heavily on my mind. Nope! For starters, I have my asthma very much under control, so it's something I have learned to live with. Rescue inhalers are mini handheld miracles. My mom also made sure I never relied on asthma as an excuse. I played just about every major sport growing up; Mom wasn't going to let it slow me down.

I look at it like this: God is my guiding light. I have complete and total faith in the Lord. Yes, I am cautious, but I am not afraid. I am aware, but I am not paralyzed. I am actually quite grateful for what COVID-19 has done for my family. I am so grateful for everything that God has given me. I have all that I need. Life is good.

Thanks to COVID-19, our family gets to spend every single day together. Our lives have really slowed down. Our world moves fast, but I have discovered so much joy in slowing down. My family has always been close, but we are even closer now than you can imagine. Last night, all six of the Martins (including Scooby) squeezed into Mom and Dad's bed for movie night. I cherish those moments. Jen reached over to grab my hand. We didn't have to say anything at all; I knew she was thinking the exact same thing. We are so lucky. It won't always be this good!

We are doing so many fun things that are simple yet so pure. One evening, the girls turned our basement into Cafe Martinez, a fine-dining establishment. Upon entry into Cafe Martinez, we were greeted by two lovely young ladies who confirmed our reservations for the evening. Detailed (handwritten) menus provided our fine dining options: cheese and crackers as an appetizer, quesadillas for the main course, and Oreo cookies for dessert. The girls even installed twinkle lights on the ceiling to make sure the atmosphere was perfect. Creative dining became a thing for us.

One evening, we ate dinner together on a plane! We were supposed to be flying to Florida to depart for a six-night cruise to the Caribbean that got canceled. Instead of going to Reagan airport, we went to our backyard to board our flight. The kids set up a few folding chairs one in front of the other, just like a Boeing 787. Drink service and meals were provided.

COVID-19 hasn't stopped the Martins from flights, fine dining, hide and seek, or the Stanley Cup finals. Directly behind our house lives the Mate family, dear friends of ours. Each night Connor Martin and Beto Mate would play against Mr. Mate and me in street hockey. This was a best of seven series that was taken very seriously. Connor and Beto deeply desired to hold up Lord Stanley. The old men versus the young bucks. The young bucks wrapped up the series in six games. Connor and Beto legitimately celebrated like they won the Stanley Cup, dumping water on each other as if it were champagne. We made them earn it, but their victory was genuine.

THE LESSON

COVID-19 forced us to slow down. Life moves so fast, but sometimes you have to slow down and just be grateful for what you have. COVID-19 could have easily put us in a bad spot mentally, but we chose to flip the script and create a few lasting memories.

COVID-19 taught me some very important lessons.

1. Slow down.
2. Keep it simple.
3. Don't let fear control you.

I am not grateful for the devastation COVID-19 will leave in its wake, but I am grateful for the lessons I have learned. I am so grateful for everything that I have and everything that God has given me. I don't take any day for granted! COVID-19 provided some great memories for the family. When you slow down, keep it simple and don't let fear control you. The world will look a little different. Even a global pandemic can't hold the Martins back. Thank you, COVID-19!

Here are nineteen fun things we did during the pandemic!

1. Nightly family dinners
2. Hide and seek
3. Coin dives in the pool
4. Played Spot It
5. Dinner at Cafe Martinez
6. Movie nights
7. Lots of bike rides
8. Booked a month-long trip to the Florida Keys (for January 2021)
9. Played with the neighbors daily
10. Jumped on the trampoline (a lot!)
11. The kids played dark tag
12. Hiked
13. Wrote this book <:
14. Learned to use Zoom

15. Played tennis
16. Ate crabs
17. Went on the boat
18. Caught fireflies
19. Ate lots of ice cream

You see, I told you COVID-19 was fun! Now, more on #18: fireflies.

CHAPTER 15

FIREFLIES

N THE EARLY part of summer, something magical happens. For a few short weeks, it's firefly season. Fireflies light the sky with their luminescent, neon-green glow. Catching fireflies has always been one of our children's favorite summertime activities. If you want to witness complete happiness, watch children catching fireflies. I am certain God created fireflies just so children can catch them.

In the early part of the fall, something magical happens. The leaves begin to change colors. Red, yellow, orange, and an abundance of variations will leave you speechless. The air is crisp, providing oxygen for the soul.

In the early part of winter, something magical happens. We get our first snowfall of the season. If you are lucky enough, the snow might be falling on a night when there is a full moon. The snowflakes reflect the moon's light, sending a rainbow of colors into the sky. Take it in. Take a walk.

In the early part of the spring, something magical happens. Flowers begin to bloom, and the birds begin to chirp. Warm breezes begin to blow, and smiles are easy to come by.

Life has seasons. Some of the seasons will be the happiest of your life. Other seasons will be the darkest of your life. I believe that through the seasons of life, God is seasoning us to become the person he put us on this earth to be. Don't try to fight it. Trust that God has a plan for you. How you choose to react to the season will be your decision. If you place your complete and total faith in God, the stress of a bad season becomes more manageable. Give your worries to him. Pray daily.

God has never failed me. He hasn't answered every prayer, but he has never failed me! I have had some very dark seasons in my life that I needed. Through the dark seasons, I learned to be the person I was meant to be. I don't know a single person who hasn't gone through some difficult seasons in life. Take comfort in knowing that you are not alone even when your season is cold and dark and feels like it will never end. Use the dark season for good in your life.

As you are well aware, this book is filled with the lessons I want you to take with you through your life. Your story will be your own, and while this might seem like a heavy chapter, it's a lesson you need to know. If you find yourself in a difficult season, take comfort knowing that there is a reason for the season. You may not fully understand why you are going through the season, but God does. I am asking that you have unconditional faith and pray.

I can share these thoughts with such confidence because God has never let me down. There were times when I felt like he did, only to later realize that he knew I needed to go through some growing pains. You will experience storms in your life that don't make sense to you, but trust me. They are part of the greater plan.

Have you ever paid attention to how fast a single day seems to go by? A day really is just a blink of an eye. Our time on earth is very short, and as you get older time does seem to go faster and faster. The season you are in might feel like it's lasting forever, but it won't. Time doesn't stand still.

I can remember like it was yesterday the first time my daughter Isabella stood on her own. I was holding her and then I ever so gently stood her up in our front yard. I let go and she did it! She stood on her own two feet for about ten seconds. That was it; that was the moment she stood on her two feet. That's how fast time goes by, and it stops for no one. Time is just one of those things that you can't stop; you can only hope that while you were on this earth you made the most of it. You can only hope that you manage to hold onto the precious moments where in a matter of seconds your children go from crawling to standing on their own two feet. Blink and you might miss it.

THE LESSON

As you continue to grow, standing on your own two feet, remember this chapter in good times and bad. Seasons provide a fresh perspective on life, even if it's not your favorite season. Every season is a growing season because you should never stop growing as a person. You guys are growing too fast. Izzy outgrew Mom yesterday.

CHAPTER 16

THE MARYLAND
BLUE CRAB

S PEAKING OF SEASONS, let me share one of my family's absolute favorites with you. If you are from Maryland, then you understand the importance of the Maryland blue crab season. If you are from Maryland and you had to choose between water to live or a bushel of crabs, it's a no-brainer. You weren't thirsty anyway! If you aren't from Maryland, it's like cheese to Wisconsin, potatoes to Idaho, peaches to Georgia, lobsters to Maine.

The sight of the crab as a meal will make most people sick to their stomach, but to Marylanders there is not a finer meal on the planet. Eating crabs is an event. Let me set the table for you.

Eating crabs is the absolute messiest meal you will ever eat in your lifetime. You don't need silverware, just a wooden knocker and your two hands. Most of the time, you will be eating them outdoors on a picnic table covered with heavy duty brown paper to protect the table and absorb the juices. You need a hard table that's well protected. Eating crabs on a nice dining room table is not recommended. I also recommend outdoor dining because the smell of old bay seasoning, butter, vinegar, and the hot steam from the crustaceans will leave quite an impression.

Let the mashing begin. You must remove the outer shell, rip the lungs off, clean out the guts, and do your best to ignore the dead crab's eyeballs that stare you down the entire time you are stuffing your face. A crab dies a miserable death. The live crab is tossed into hot steam until it is lifeless. Crab picking, or banging hard shells as the locals say, is a full-contact sport and is not for the faint of heart. However, inside the crab you will find a great treasure: the meat is the best on the planet.

When you sit down to eat crabs, you should never wear white clothing, since it will certainly get soiled. Make sure you aren't going out in public afterward, as you will be dirty and smell. When banging hardshells, you must always be on guard. At any given moment during the feast, a cousin, aunt, uncle, or family friend might accidentally send a piece of shell flying in your direction. *Might* isn't the right word to use. You *will* get hit with flying crab shell while banging crabs. You will also likely come away with a few battle wounds. You know the sting you experience after you pour peroxide on a cut? Crabs are pointy and sharp, so you will cut your hand. The salt and vinegar will replicate the feeling of peroxide. Marylanders work through this pain with a smile.

Crab season typically begins around Memorial Day and officially ends on Labor Day. I say officially because Marylanders like to extend the season as long as possible sometimes stretching into November. Crab season is more than a meal, though. It signals the start of summer. Maryland summers are filled with sunshine and happiness. Our winters can be a bit chilly, so when crab season kicks off, the fun begins. Summer fun is about watching sunsets on the water, it's about long days and warm breezes. It's about jumping on the boat, sitting on the back porch, spending time with aunts, uncles, cousins, grandmas, and grandads. And, of course, it means football season is around the corner. Crabs and football. That's what Maryland is about (guess the movie that line is from).

Marylanders learn to eat crabs at a young age. When you are a kid, the crab meat is picked for you by mom and dad, but that only lasts a season or two. If you are old enough to walk, then you are old enough to pick your own crab. The love of crabs is handed down from each generation. It's like a sacred rite of passage. Eating crabs is more than just a meal. It's a sacred tradition; it's family bonding time.

Nothing brings a family together more than fresh crabs. If you want to see relatives you haven't heard from in a while, invite them over for crabs and see what happens. Eating crabs takes several hours and no one eats just one. If you want to know what's happening in the world, just sit down at a crab table with relatives. Welcome or unwelcome, you are going to hear lots of opinions about what's right and what's wrong with the world. Marylanders don't break bread together. They bang crab shells together.

THE LESSON

I absolutely love crabs, if you can't tell already, but I want you to know the importance of handing down family traditions. I want you to know the importance of spending time with your relatives. You need to know who your family is. You need to know what's happening in their worlds. We lead busy lives and catching up with all of your family might be difficult, but make sure you do it. It's equally as important to them as it is to you. It's important to keep traditions alive. It's important to keep families in touch.

It's not about eating crabs; it's about spending time with family! OK, maybe it is also about eating crabs—they are that good—but don't lose the message here.

Create traditions, create memories, and spend time with your family. You will create memories that you will never forget. You will never forget crabs on Grandma's back porch with the cousins.

Grandma's Porch on the Patuxent River

CHAPTER 17

THE FIVE-GALLON BUCKET

W HEN I WAS child, one of my favorite memories was spending the night at Grandma's house. My grandparents lived in a blue-collar community just outside of Washington, DC. Grandma and Grandad Martin moved closer to the big city from rural Virginia because they understood DC offered work, DC offered opportunity. Grandad Martin drove for Yellow Cab and Grandma worked as a waitress at a cocktail lounge.

As a young child, staying at Grandma's house was always a treat. The days were filled with good old-fashioned fun. I would play outside all day with some of the kids from the neighborhood followed by an evening playing gin rummy (card game) and watching *The Wizard of Oz*. On Sunday morning, Grandad would make a big old-fashioned country breakfast—country ham and fried potatoes that I still crave to do this day. Grandad would use an old-fashioned skillet, tossing in some potatoes and onions with plenty of salt and pepper. The entire house would smell so good. After our country breakfast, Grandad and I would head off to the bowling alley.

Bowling was our ritual, and it was always understood that's what we would do after breakfast. However, before heading to the bowling alley, Grandad always asked me a simple question, "What's on your mind?" I knew that was my cue to tell him we should go bowling. I can't remember a single time when he didn't ask me the question before we would go. I now realize many years later that his question was by design. He was teaching me to say what's on mind. My grandad and I loved duckpin bowling, a variation of traditional bowling that involves smaller balls without holes. We took bowling very seriously. We had our own shoes and custom balls with our initials. Grandad Martin's initials were J. E. M.: James Edwards Martin. My son's middle name is James after Grandad Martin. I enjoy calling my son James because it reminds me of Grandad Martin.

I never got bored at Grandma's house. It was always easy to find something to occupy my time. Just a few blocks from Grandma's house was a mini shopping center that included a grocery store and an arcade. This combination of grocery store and arcade turned out to be a match made in heaven. Adjacent to my grandparents' home lived Scott, who was my age and always looking for fun. Our typical day involved playing one-on-one tackle football followed by a trip to the grocery store. What would two eight-year-old boys be doing at a grocery store, you might ask? The arcade games required quarters and the grocery store provided the perfect opportunity to earn a few. We loved going to the arcade; however, this wasn't an adventure my grandparents were going to fund.

Scott and I figured out a way to make money on our own. Okay, truth be told, Scott already had this plan working, but he was happy to include me. The grocery store became our gold mine. One by one, old ladies would exit the store with carts full of groceries—groceries that Scott and I would happily load into their cars. As you can imagine, we didn't officially work for the grocery store, but let's just say we were independent contractors.

My first paying job was at the age of eight. We worked for tips. The average tip per cart was about twenty-five cents. Scott and I were wise beyond our years, realizing that if we asked the ladies if they would like help loading their groceries, it opened up the conversation for a no. We adjusted our game plan and just started helping them without asking. This approach just about guaranteed a tip was coming our way. In the early eighties, twenty-five cents was good enough for one arcade game. We would load about five or six cars then head straight to the arcade. Rinse and repeat, we wore that arcade out. We sure do live in a different world today. There's not a chance in hell I would let my kids load groceries for strangers. Isn't it funny how we learn certain lessons in life? My love of entrepreneurship began at the age of eight!

I learned early on in my life that making money involved work. This is a lesson that was handed down from my parents. During summer break from school, I would occasionally go to work with my dad. My dad was a one-man-band plumber who worked in the city, and Mom was a paralegal downtown. My parents both worked hard to provide for my sister and me. The plumbing business was reliable, but reliable doesn't mean easy. Most of the accounts my dad worked were in the impoverished apartment complexes of Washington, DC. These communities were dangerous, filled with crime, drugs, and violence. We had to make sure we were always aware of our surroundings!

My primary job was to carry the five-gallon bucket of tools. It was a two-handed carry, since the bucket was full and very heavy. I would lug the bucket up and down the stairs on hot summer days. The buildings we worked in weren't equipped with elevators or air-conditioned hallways, and DC is *hot* in the summer. Make no mistake, a plumber's work is not for those with queasy stomachs. Our jobs frequently involved plunging toilets. When you plunge a toilet, it's because the toilet won't flush. If the toilet didn't flush, that usually means poop would still be floating. There's nothing better than plunging a stranger's poop that's been lingering around for days. I am joking, of course. Who you gonna call? Not ghostbusters, but the plumber. The smell of other people's—makes me want to vomit to this day. Remember, AC wasn't an option, and the heat had the tendency to amplify the smell.

The lessons I learned working with my dad on hot summer days proved to be invaluable.

- Lesson #1: I don't want to be a plumber when I grow up.
- Lesson # 2: Do hard work.
- Lesson #3: Be aware of your surroundings *at all times.*

I am so thankful my parents made sure I understood the value of hard work. Work ethic is a valuable skill in any profession and oftentimes is a requirement for success. Hard work also comes with a great sense of satisfaction, a great sense of accomplishment. It's that feeling of "I earned it!" When you earn it, whatever it is has more meaning and more value to you.

THE LESSON

Listen to the stories of success that are all around you. People get excited when they share their stories of success, especially if they earned it. You don't hear the same sense of pride when someone was given something. You don't ever hear, "I was given this, and I am so proud of myself for not earning it!"

I have great respect for how hard both of my parents worked to provide for my sister and me. They both worked diligently and earned everything they have. Just know that to reach the top of any stairs, you are going to need to carry a five-gallon bucket on hot summer days and you might need to plunge a few toilets.

CHAPTER 18

THE CANDY SHOP

LIVE IN A house with a bunch of salesmen. I guess this is an environment my wife and I have created, since we are both entrepreneurs. My kids are always interested in conversations about what they could sell or things they can do to earn money. My children definitely aren't afraid to go door to door to pedal their product. Have you ever had someone knock on your door to see if you would be interested in purchasing a homemade potholder? Thankfully, our neighbors find our traveling salesman cute, but make no mistake my children are on a mission.

On any given Saturday in our neighborhood, some sort of hustle is likely happening. The services or goods offered covers the full gamut from leaf collection to car washing. My son recently covered the neighborhood in flyers to inform everyone about his new rollerblading business. If your child needs rollerblading lessons, Connor is your dude. My daughter Izzy recently planned a carnival, complete with games, cotton candy, and hot dogs. The games required tickets, tickets that cost money. I love the enthusiasm my kids have for making a buck.

Isabella has a good chance to create financial wealth in her lifetime. She gets it. She reads books about money and understands the basics of what you can do with the money you earn. At the age of ten, she could recite the four things you can do with money.

1. Save
2. Invest
3. Spend
4. Give

She fully understands the difference between spending and investing. Izzy purchased her first stock at the age of ten (Target TGT) and doubled her money two years later.

My children have discovered that you can turn your passions into a business. Isabella loves candy; she definitely has her mother's sweet tooth. Just for fun, we occasionally call her Buddy, from the holiday movie *Elf*. If Izzy could put syrup on her pasta, she absolutely would do so. Our kitchen has become her laboratory. To give you some insight, one of her most recent experiments was chocolate chip Oreo cookies, not chocolate chip and Oreo cookies, but rather an Oreo cookie baked inside a chocolate chip cookie. As much as Izzy loves eating chocolate, she equally loves selling her products.

My wife and I encourage and support our budding entrepreneurs. In an effort to teach Izzy the basics of business, my wife and I agreed to let Izzy sell a few pieces of candy to her friends at school. Our goal was to teach her about profit and loss. You know the basics: if you buy a candy bar for $1 and sell it for $2, you made $1 in profit. What started out as a simple experiment turned out to be a legitimate candy-selling service. Izzy quickly learned that selling candy to a bunch of middle schoolers is like shooting fish in a barrel. Izzy's business quickly became profitable. In a few short weeks, she was netting a $100 a week from her candy business. She was running out of inventory fast, which required Jen and I to make nightly trips to Target to replenish it.

As an unforeseen bonus, Izzy also began working on her social media marketing strategy. She started pre-selling the candy on Snapchat! She quickly learned the power of visual marketing. One quick pic of a Ring Pop on Snap was definitely enough to capture a sixth-grader's attention.

Izzy learned that Target had cheaper Pop Rocks than the Hollin Hall Variety Store (a throwback from the old dime store days). Izzy had this business down to a science. Eventually, Jen and I had to shut the business down because we figured it was only a matter of time before we were going to receive a call from the school.

I am so proud of Izzy. She knows more about the basics of money at age twelve than most adults. According to Google, 75 percent of people in the United States live paycheck to paycheck, and that's not only a problem, it's scary! One of the ways to solve this problem is through a simple concept known as delayed gratification. We live in an instant world; we want things now. But *now* is not how wealth is typically created.

Jen and I work hard to teach our children this concept of delayed gratification. It has been scientifically proven that delayed gratification comes with many rewards. A 1972 study led by Stanford psychologist Walter Mischel used children and marshmallows to test the potential benefits of delayed gratification. Children were offered one marshmallow or pretzel stick. They were told they could have one marshmallow or pretzel stick immediately or if they waited about fifteen minutes they could have multiple marshmallows or pretzel sticks. Years later, a follow-up study concluded that those children who held out for multiple marshmallows or pretzel sticks seemed to have better SAT scores, body mass indexes, and other life measures.

THE LESSON

Money is such an interesting topic because I am certain that money doesn't guarantee happiness. Happiness is found in the heart, not in the wallet. Money will expose you, for better or worse. Greed is a bad thing. However, money in the hands of good people is a good thing. Good people tend to do good things with their money, helping make the world a better place. I believe creating wealth is a good thing, especially if you choose to do good things with the wealth you create.

Wealth can provide peace of mind; wealth can create opportunities. Wealth can also destroy you. Material things are fine, but I crave experiences, and I pray that I can make a difference in the world with whatever wealth I create. If you choose to build wealth, make sure you don't sacrifice your soul. Stay true to your core values and do good with what God has given you. And if you want a candy bar, hit up Snapchat. Izzy has you covered!

CHAPTER 19

GEORGE BUSH

CORE VALUES ARE so important to me. I never want to compromise my own values for success in any way shape or form. Life will certainly tempt you with what feels like opportunity if you are willing to flex a little on your value system. When this temptation comes into your world, reject it immediately. In life most of us are prewired with a moral compass of what's right and what's wrong; I call it my gut instinct. One of my favorite examples of a leader who stayed true to their core values was the late president George H. W. Bush who passed away in 2018. This letter resurfaced after his passing and was written as advice for you young people.

- Don't get down when your life takes a bad turn. Out of adversity comes challenge and often success.
- Don't blame others for your setbacks.
- When things go well, always give credit to others.
- Don't talk all the time. Listen to your friends and mentors and learn from them.

- Don't brag about yourself. Let others point out your virtues, your strong points.
- Give someone else a hand. When a friend is hurting, show that friend you care.
- Nobody likes an overbearing big shot.
- As you succeed, be kind to people. Thank those who help you along the way.
- Don't be afraid to shed a tear when your heart is broken because a friend is hurting.
- Say your prayers!

These words were written as advice for young people; however, I am certain everyone reading can find the advice useful. I love the simplicity and the sincerity of each message. This simple letter tells me quite a bit about #41's character and his core values.

Don't get down when your life takes a bad turn. Out of adversity comes challenge and often success. Dad's view: Life is going to take a bad turn on you. Bad turns are part of life, but every bad turn should be viewed as an opportunity to create a better version of yourself. It won't always be easy to see the opportunity in the moment, but give it time.

Don't blame others for your setbacks. Dad's view: Even if the setback is caused by someone else, don't blame them. Forgive them even if they don't ask and move forward.

Playing the blame game will only slow you down. At my office I keep an oversized wooden sign. In big red letters one of my favorite words is written: NEXT. Get good at NEXT; you will need it.

When things go well, always give credit to others. Dad's view: No one succeeds alone. Never. Never. Never forget that.

Don't talk all the time. Listen to your friends and mentors and learn from them. Dad's view: Practice listening. It's a learned skill that is powerful. Pick a few people to be your mentor; always be a student. Your mentors don't have to be someone you have a close personal relationship with. Never stop learning, never! Learning new things is fun and good for the brain. Mom tells me I have too many hobbies. I totally disagree. <:

Don't brag about yourself. Let others point out your virtues, your strong points. Dad's view: I can't stand people who brag about themselves. It's a big turnoff for me. It shows insecurity and a lack of confidence. You can share your successes when asked, but do it in a humble manner.

Give someone else a hand. When a friend is hurting, show that friend you care. Dad's view: Friends won't always tell you when they are hurting. Being a good friend requires asking. Sometimes their pain will be obvious but sometimes not. Showing someone you care means a lot; people don't do this enough.

Nobody likes an overbearing big shot. Dad's view: The most powerful position in the world is the president of the United States. I believe #41 lived by the advice he offered. He wasn't an overbearing big shot. If he can do it, so can you.

As you succeed, be kind to people. Thank those who help you along the way. Dad's view: The impact you have on others is much greater than you realize. Use it for good. Kindness feels good. When you're feeling down, do something kind for someone else and see what happens.

Don't be afraid to shed a tear when your heart is broken because a friend is hurting. Dad's view: I am not good at this one, but shedding a tear is a sign of strength, not weakness.

Say your prayers! Dad's view: This has always worked for me. Even the prayers that aren't answered seem to have a way of working out for the better. Trust that the Lord has a plan for you. He does!

CHAPTER 20

MARLAN FOREST

TALKING ABOUT #41 has me feeling patriotic. I place my hand over my heart when I hear "The Star-Spangled Banner." Our family lives in a suburb just outside of Washington, DC, known as Marlan Forest. Our little neighborhood is eight miles from the front door of the United States Capitol, but you would never know it. City life is busy, but our suburban oasis is a refreshing throwback. Most of the homes were built in the early 1960s, and if you ask its residents, many will confirm that Marlan Forest is the absolute best neighborhood in the world.

I often describe our community as Sesame Street because at any given time you might have twelve kids playing tag on your front lawn. I have tried many times to keep a lush green front lawn, but for some reason I just can't do it!

I have had more than one neighbor share with me that the only way they will leave the neighborhood is feet first. Think about that for a second and you will get it!

Our neighborhood has established many traditions over the years, but perhaps the most coveted happens on

Independence Day. On July 4, Marlan Forest hosts its very own parade. To the children of Marlan Forest, our parade might as well be the Macy's Thanksgiving Day parade. All the children take their roles very seriously. Days in advance of the parade, they begin decorating their bikes. Each bike is meticulously prepared with flags, ribbons, lights, and anything else red, white, and blue that will fit. The neighborhood kids make the parade so very special. Just about every house in the neighborhood proudly flies Old Glory. Faces are painted, and you will find smiles in every direction. Our parade route is one square block, lasting about a quarter of a mile. I believe the founding fathers of our country would be proud of our parade.

Jennifer, Isabella, Riley, Connor, and Dad

One of my favorite feelings after a long day in the city is the drive south along the George Washington Parkway adjacent to the Potomac River, a route President George Washington took many times, to his home, Mount Vernon Estate. I don't take my ride home for granted. I know how lucky I am to live in the United States of America. An overwhelming sense of pride comes over me as I realize how fortunate I am to lead the life I do. I am grateful for the country we live in. I am grateful for those who came before me and sacrificed their lives for this great country we call home. God bless the USA. As with all countries, we have our problems that will always need to be addressed, but in my humble opinion we live in the greatest country in the world.

This is the country we live in and I am proud to be a part of it. Both of my grandfathers served our country, including one purple heart recipient who battled on the beaches of Normandy.

It's important for my kids to understand the sacrifices that were made and the price that was paid for freedom. I want you to take great pride in our country and never stop fighting for her independence. In your lifetime, you will experience what seems like a country divided, a government divided, but don't mistake what you are experiencing. It's called freedom and many have given their lives to protect it. Never take it for granted. We should always strive to protect what we have and simultaneously work to make our nation even better.

Our country is like no other, a true melting pot filled with people from all over the world, which means varying opinions will be readily available. Our country is not and will never be perfect, as we definitely have our flaws, but it is a country I am very proud to live in. It's a country that your relatives fought to defend.

Take pride in the USA. God bless the USA. As debates about right and wrong surface, understand that this is how our country works. It was designed that way. You won't agree with everything and you should stand up for what you believe in. That's a right granted to you as a US citizen.

THE LESSON

This country is worth fighting for and our freedom today came at a price. Our freedom tomorrow will also come at a price. I want you to know how proud I am of our great country. I also want to tell those reading right now if you wish to do harm to our great nation, please remove yourself.

CHAPTER 21

ARNOLD PALMER

I AM FASCINATED BY people; people have always piqued my curiosity. People are worth taking the time to get to know.

I want to share one of my favorite moments from when I was a young sports reporter in Augusta, Georgia. I was covering the Masters in 2001 and I was running the camera for George Eskola, the local reporter who had been around Augusta forever. I was green. George, however, likely started covering the masters before I was born. George was a recognizable face to those who lived in Augusta, but beyond the city limits, very few people would have any idea of who George Eskola was or where he worked.

Just being on the grounds of Augusta National Golf Club is an amazing feeling. I grew up my entire life watching the Masters. The second Sunday of April has always held a special place in my heart. Amen corner (holes 11, 12, and 13) is one the most sacred places on earth, and I could hardly believe that I was covering the Masters. It was surreal. Each morning before the start of the tournament I would arrive before the patrons and walk the grounds just to take in the experience. It was a breathtaking experience to say the least. I was in my early twenties, chasing a dream and covering the masters.

George and I were waiting outside the clubhouse for the King to come out. Golf fans know who I am talking about: the late Arnold Palmer. Waiting for Arnold to come out at Augusta is like waiting to see the pope. Arnold is to golf what Michael Jordan is to basketball! His popularity literally helped globalize the game of golf. During his prime, whether you were a golf fan or not, you knew Arnold Palmer. Arnold Palmer transcended the game of golf.

George casually said to me, "Let's go over here and grab Arnold for a sound bite [quick interview]." My mind was racing and heart pounding, I was about to be steps away from the King. I was certain George was a little overzealous with his ambitions of grabbing a quick second with the King, but I went along with the plan. We were just going to walk over and grab the King Arnold Palmer. Right. No chance! Everyone in small-town Augusta knows George, but no chance the King knows George. Or so I thought.

Arnold walked out of the clubhouse and the mad dash to get close began. It was a frenzy. It's elbow to elbow and every reporter/cameraman fights for inches of real estate. The King walked out of the clubhouse and right up to George Eskola. "Hi, George, how you doing?" Holy bleep the King just walked right up to the local reporter in a small market and said hello! It was on this day that I learned a valuable life lesson that I will never forget. People are just people. Arnold fully understood this, which is why I believe people were drawn to him. His fans were known as Arnie's Army, and they loved their king.

Arnold understood he was a person just like you and me. Arnold also had a keen sense of his influence on others. Despite being a global figure, Arnold was humble and kind and used his influence for good. I watched a documentary of Arnold after his passing in 2016 that confirmed what I already knew to be true: Arnold was a good soul. Arnold used his celebrity for the good it could bring and simultaneously understood that people are just people regardless of their status.

This is a lesson my kids haven't fully grasped yet, but I am working on it. Currently my youngest daughter Riley believes that Disney's Dove Cameron walks on water. Dove is the lead character in the show *Liv and Maddie*. I have watched more episodes of *Liv and Maddie* then I would like to admit.

THE LESSON

People are just people regardless of their status. They have problems and challenges just like we do. Use your influence for good and always treat others with kindness. Your influence on others is much greater than you know, regardless of your own social or economic status. Be like Arnold, who on a special day in April 2001 walked right up to George Eskola and a young kid with big aspirations. Quick sidenote: I also have a story about Tiger Woods from that same tournament you should ask me about.

CHAPTER 22

MOM'S VIEW

S PEAKING OF PEOPLE, I asked mom to contribute a chapter in this book. I gave Mom a blank slate and said to write about anything she so desired. She chose people as her topic.

Jason asked me to contribute to his book and suggested I could discuss whatever topic I wanted to. Since our kids will see this at some point, I decided to keep it clean. :) I also wanted to share some insight with them that will hopefully help them down the road and perhaps you too. . . .

Barbara Streisand sings that "people who need people are the luckiest people in the world," and I'm not sure I fully agree with her. Then there is a saying, I'm sure you've heard it: "People, you can't live with them and you can't live without them." I, for one, can tell you there will definitely be some that you can live without!

The question I pose to you is, "What kind of people person are you?" Do you surround yourself with people who only agree with your point of view or ones who challenge you? Ones who make you laugh or ones who need constant nurturing?

In life, you're going to cross paths with many people from all different walks of life. In fact, the current world population is estimated at 7.8 billion. That is a whole lot of fish in the sea!

People relationships are tricky. They can make you laugh, make you ugly cry ("face crumples up and mascara streaming down your face" type of cry), bring you joy, cause sadness, make you happy, make you think, let you be silly, let you escape reality at times, and/or let you be you.

There are also people in life who are constantly negative, jealous, consistently lying, condescending, and/or make you feel worthless. These are people who aren't just having a bad day, but who are consistently like this. In this instance, they are more than likely dealing with their own internal stuff, and it's not you. Try to stay away from them or keep them at a very long arm's length if you can't avoid them!

People relationships can take up a large chunk of the bandwidth in your brain (i.e., how much you can deal with/comprehend at one time), the bandwidth that you also use to handle all of your own feelings and the things you want to achieve in life. If you give up too much of that bandwidth to others, you will miss out on things for yourself. I'm not saying become a selfish a-hole. I'm saying keep track of how much of you that you're giving to help others manage their stuff. If you find yourself snapping at a lot at people or losing your temper easily, you may want to step back and evaluate what is taking up your bandwidth.

Some people will leave a big impression, even if you only have a brief encounter with them, and some will leave no impression at all except that their face looks familiar. This is not groundbreaking news; it's a reminder.

A reminder that you need to treat people the way you want to be treated. A reminder that the world is small and you may end up crossing paths with people at various points in your life, so don't burn your bridges. A reminder to be the same person both on and offline. Do not get behind your keyboard and say something that you wouldn't say to their face!

Also, when you cross these paths, don't just take the safe one. If you constantly surround yourself with people who only agree with you, you may become complacent in life. You may not push yourself to achieve your dreams. You may have regrets and too many "what ifs" if you go this way.

You also don't have to take the path that looks like it leads into a spooky forest that you may or may not come out of. :) Yes, be a calculated risk taker and push yourself, at times, out of your comfort zone. Be the first to introduce yourself at an event or you might miss an opportunity.

Last of all, give people the benefit of the doubt and, if needed, a chance for a second impression. I can come across as brash with my "what you see is what you get" attitude and if it wasn't for second impressions, I wouldn't have some of my closest friends in my life! So thank you to them—they know who they are. :)

CHAPTER 23

JOHN COLEMAN

S OME PEOPLE WILL have a powerful impact on your life. I think of it like this: they can be a propeller, or they can be an anchor. Anchors are the people who hold you down, keeping you from moving forward. Propellers support speed, growth, momentum, and progress. I prefer to surround myself with propellers. My professional propeller and good friend is John Coleman. (Hey, John, I bet you didn't think you would get your own chapter in this book!) You are that important to me, my friend, and I am grateful for the impact you have had on my life. Thank you.

John Coleman was someone I wanted to be in business with. I have an entrepreneurial spirit, which is a blessing and a curse. It's exciting and stressful at the same time. The single most important lesson I have learned as an entrepreneur is that my success is directly linked to people. When I surround myself with the right people, anything is possible. This might sound a bit selfish, so let me further clarify. The people game is a two-way street. You can't just surround yourself with the right people and watch the magic happen. You must care for them the same way they care for you. You must pour into them the same way they pour into you. I care deeply about John's success as a person and as an entrepreneur. If he wins, I win. It's that simple. I find great satisfaction in helping people achieve what they want from life. Do you understand what I am trying to say? It's not about me; it's about them. A rising tide lifts all boats and I want to be the rising tide lifting up everyone who is important to me. John Coleman is so much more to me than a propeller. He and his wife, Julia, are some of my favorite people in the world.

Jason Martin and John Coleman

As an entrepreneur, I face many challenges. One of my many challenges is that I am always thinking about different businesses I can start. Other entrepreneurs will know exactly what I am talking about right now because it's an urge that's hard to resist. Let me give you an example. A friend of mine, Jack Gorman, needed to create some income as his existing employer was anything but reliable. I knew Jack was a good dude and I wanted to help him, as well as scratch my own entrepreneurial itch. I had a few ideas about things we could sell, and Jack had the creative/editorial talent to pull it off. Jack Gorman is an aspiring movie producer, so we decided to start a video production company targeting small business owners. We had created a ninety-second promotional video for the Jason Martin Group (real estate team) and decided it was a product all small businesses could use, so 1790 Media was launched. We had sharp business cards and a cool name. We were ready to set the world on fire. Jack Gorman suggested we talk to our mutual acquaintance John Coleman to help launch 1790. At the time John was looking for additional streams of income.

The plan was to reach out to small businesses and offer them the opportunity to do a one- to two-minute video promo of their business. We needed someone who was willing to get face-to-face with business owners because we were certain we had the product they needed. John Coleman literally went door to door looking for business. Our plan was totally going to work . . . until it didn't! I think we might have sold a total of five videos.

1790 Media was a bust and a monumental win at the same time. 1790 is the reason John Coleman entered my professional world. I originally told myself that if 1790 could financially support Jack, it would be a win. I was coming from a good spot with good intentions, and I believe that's why John came into my world. I don't want to give myself too much credit, but one of my strengths is realizing what talent looks like. In case you're not sure, talent looks like John Coleman. He was willing to go door to door for a startup that didn't even have a real business plan. John had drive, hustle, grit, willingness, integrity, and whatever other adjectives you'd use to describe someone you want to be in business with, and I knew it.

One of the many lessons I have learned the hard way over the years is that, above all else, you'd better make sure the person you are going into business with matches your core values. My professional core values are basic: (1) Integrity; (2) Client first; and (3) Have fun. John absolutely checked every one of those boxes. Do you think John is a propeller? I have now been in business with John for almost five years and made him a partner in the Jason Martin Group in 2019, an organization that has sold well over $400 million dollars' worth of real estate.

THE LESSON

My wife and I love John and Julia beyond the business. We love them as people. Who do you have in your life you can say the same about? If you really want your world to change, you will need propellers. It can't just be about you and your needs; you also need to pour into the other person. Don't be selfish. You authentically need to give back to the propellers in your life for the right reasons. If you can't add value to them, then it's a one-way relationship and one-way relationships have limited potential. You should LOVE the people who matter most to you and put their dreams above your own ambitions.

CHAPTER 24

QUESTIONS

HAVE A FEW questions for you, and I hope that you will pause and think about them after reading. Where do I want to be in life? Am I the best version of myself possible? What would happen if? Don't just keep reading. Put the book down and answer those questions. What did you come up with?

Here's another question for you, What's the difference between you and Warren Buffett? The obvious answer is "your bank accounts," as he is considered one of the most successful investors in the world. The gap between his bank account and mine is quite large—Grand Canyon large. If I wanted to be like Warren Buffett, what would it take? I call that the gap. The gap is the distance between where you are and where you want to be. To close the gap, we need to start asking ourselves some questions. What habits has Warren created that I can learn from? Apparently, he reads for five to six hours per day. He also recently donated $2.9 billion to charity. Remember earlier I mentioned creating wealth for the good it can bring to the world? Warren clearly exemplifies that.

When you start asking questions, you begin to approach what I call the starting line. Everyone at every level begins at the starting line. Your race distance might only be a lap or two or perhaps it's a marathon, but regardless of the distance, everyone begins their journey in the exact same place as you: the starting line.

You and I will each approach the starting line with different abilities. I might be able to run a seven-minute mile and perhaps you can run a six-minute mile. I don't want your pace to deter me from running my race. Don't forget the classic fable "The Tortoise and the Hare." I desire to learn from those who can run faster than I can, but, remember, it's your race and you decide where your finish line will be.

Have you ever envied another person, wishing you had what they have? Thinking they have it so good? Let me stop you right here, because regardless of economic or social status, people are just people, remember? We each face our own unique set of challenges in life and NO ONE is exempt. If we are just people and we all face challenges in life and we all begin at a starting line, then what really sets people apart? The secret lies within the question.

Highly successful people not only ask questions, but they also ask the *right* questions. One of the most important questions is this: what's the difference between where

I am and where I want to be? They ask it and fervently seek the answer with the understanding that it's likely a process. Truth be told, we don't all have the ability to be the next Steve Jobs. However, we do have way more potential than we can even imagine.

Steve Jobs said, "Technology is nothing. What's important is that you have faith in people that they're basically good and smart." I, too, have great faith in people, and I believe your journey begins when you ask yourself the right questions. A fun pattern starts to evolve when you ask yourself the right questions. You begin winning races! If you win enough races (maybe even just finish them), you might become great! At a bare minimum, you will be able to say you gave it a go. You will never have a chance to finish the race if you don't step up to the starting line. Grab your running shoes and start asking questions!

In my previous career as a sports anchor and in my current career as a realtor, I get to meet plenty of interesting people, people I love asking questions of. Here are a few of my favorites.

Jason: Michael, do you see any of yourself in some of the younger guys on the team?
Michael: No, not really.

The Michael I am talking about is Michael Jordan. Jordan announced his return to basketball in 2001 and played for the Washington Wizards, who held their training camp in his hometown Wilmington, North Carolina, where I was the main sports anchor. As Michael answered, he tossed me a big wink and smile. His answer told me what I already believed to be true: his competitive spirit is off the charts, and even late in his career, he still believed he was one of the greatest in the world.

Jason: What sets a professional athlete apart?
Gary: When a professional athlete is backed up against the wall, they have this unique ability to move forward.

That was Gary Clark, who won two Super Bowls with the Washington Football Team. I conducted this interview long after I exited the sports industry. Since I still love learning from people, I host my own podcast. Check out the interview with Gary on my YouTube channel, "People Passion Power with Jason Martin." You should watch the full interview and listen to all the lessons Gary shares. To date, Gary was one of my favorite interviews. I have rewatched it many times as I continue to learn from his words of wisdom.

Jason: It appears you have everything you need in life, why congress now?

Mitt: I feel like the country needs stability and that's something I believe I can help with.

I was lucky enough to spend time with Ann and Mitt Romney after the Utah senate seat was decided. The Romneys are two very amazing people that I am grateful to have spent time with. Mitt was kind enough to host me for breakfast in the Senate Dining Room. It's Washington's most exclusive dining room and it was a very special treat for me. I had lots of questions for Senator Romney, who graciously shared his time and knowledge with me. I captured lots of nuggets from this meeting that I am happy to share with you—but only if you *ask*.

THE LESSON

Does everything begin with a question? Questions you ask yourself and of others will help determine your future. Don't ever let fear prohibit you from asking questions. Learn to ask good questions. Your success depends on it. You might only be one question away from changing your entire life!

CHAPTER 25

WALKS WITH
MY WIFE

HAVE SO MUCH to be grateful for. I am grateful that I have everything I need in life. I have a warm home, a loving wife, and three children (and a dog) whom I love more than anything in the world. I really don't need anything else. When you can view the world through this lens, it keeps everything in perspective. When life gets stressful, I remind myself that I have everything I need. This simple reminder allows me to clear the clutter in my brain and lets my brain know that my life is good. I should stop stressing about the things that don't matter.

Just sharing what I am grateful for gives me peace of mind. I am not a cognitive psychologist, but I can tell you that a shift happens almost instantaneously when I share what I am grateful for. Every Monday during my organizational meetings, the very first thing we do to start the new week is share our gratitude. I know the effect gratitude has on me, and now I also get to watch the impact it has on others.

Sharing genuine gratitude is a natural way to relieve stress. When I ask people each week to share what they are grateful for, I don't give any stipulations. They can share whatever they like. Do you want to know what most people's gratitude revolves around? People. About ninety percent of the time, gratitude revolves around other people. I don't hear people say, "I am so grateful for my shiny new watch." Instead, I hear them say, "I am grateful for my neighbor who . . ."

Gratitude doesn't have to be complicated. In fact, it should be simple. We have enough things in life that are complicated.

I am grateful for summer evenings, that perfect time of day when the sun has an amazing glow, the heat has cooled, and a soft, warm breeze hits your skin.

I am also grateful for sunrises. A few times a week, I will drive my twins to school, which starts at 7:00 a.m.! I think that's a little early for them, but when school starts that early, you can catch the sunrise. The neighborhood we live in sits above the Potomac River. I know exactly where the best sunrise viewing area is located, so when I drive the kids to school, we take the sunrise route. They have no idea that I take this route on purpose, but I do!

I am grateful for walks with my wife. It's a sacred space where we can share what's on our minds, where we can dream and talk over our challenges. It's a space where we can get away from the kids for a few minutes (parents need this).

I am grateful for the Mount Vernon trail. When the world is weighing heavy on my mind, I jump on the trail for a run or bike ride.

I am grateful for the holiday season. I love when Mom Mom and Pop Pop come and stay for a few weeks. We make lots of cookies, watch lots of movies, take lots of naps, and usually stay in our pajamas for a few weeks.

I am grateful for Christmas Eves at Grandma's house. This is one of Grandma's favorite days of the year. It makes her so happy that it makes me happy.

I am grateful for Maryland blue crabs. My entire family lives for crabs in the summer. Every summer, we jump on Grandad's boat to go bang some hard shells.

I am grateful for the Thanksgiving trips we would take to South Carolina to visit my wife's late grandma, Gigi.

I am grateful for the magical color of trees during the fall. The foliage lasts only two or three weeks, but it is truly magical.

I am grateful for pumpkin patches. Big orange pumpkins that become scary jack-o'-lanterns. Pumpkins have such a distinct smell; I can smell it now as I describe them.

I am grateful for the ocean and the sound of the waves.

I am grateful for good sleep and the way it makes me feel the next day.

I am grateful for exercise and the way it releases stress.

I am grateful for people, experiences, and memories.

I am most grateful for my family and the memories we have created. I hope these memories will stay with me until the day I die. I could go on and on with things I am grateful for.

THE LESSON: BE GRATEFUL

When you are in the moment, give thanks to God for what you are experiencing. He gifted you that moment. I am grateful to be alive. I am even grateful for the word *gratitude*. Don't ever take for granted the good things in life that are all around you. Keep it simple. Keep things in perspective no matter what season of life you are in. You will ALWAYS have something in your life to be grateful for, but sometimes you have to slow down and think about it. When you are having a bad day, just think of a few things or people you are grateful for and see what happens.

I am grateful that you are reading this book!

CHAPTER 26

THOUGHTS
FROM DAD

A COLLECTION OF MY own thoughts is as valuable as a pot of gold to me. Your life experiences will be one of your greatest teachers. Take notes or, better yet, start journaling so you can learn from yourself. Here are some of my motivational thoughts I have captured in my journal over the years. I realized in reflection the thoughts were written to inspire me, to motivate me. I think it has worked!

APRIL 2012

I am going to change the negative past habits of my life. To do so, I will need to take control of the actions I take and with whom I choose to spend time. I will control my mind and not let my mind control me. My mind is my servant, not my master. I will only focus on four things: faith, family, work, and health. If it doesn't involve any of these four, forget about it.

MARCH 11, 2013

To achieve what I want to in my career and life takes devotion. Meaning I need to attack each day with energy. To do so I need to be asleep by 10:00 p.m. To sleep by 10:00, I need to eat right and drink plenty of water. Most successful people go to sleep early, exercise, and watch their diet. Good living means good thinking, and it leads to more quality time with the family.

MAY 28, 2013

I have decided that I can achieve greatness. The older I get, the wiser I become. If I only listen to myself a little more.

AUGUST 10, 2013

I am a very lucky man. God has treated me very well, and I am grateful for all the wonderful gifts he has given me. Some days I feel like the luckiest man alive.

JANUARY 26, 2014

Every so often your life comes into harmony. I mean spiritual, marriage, kids, and professional. I am headed into one of those grooves and it's helping me grow as a person. I have accepted/ realized that I don't have time for too many things in life other than those most important to me.

MAY 26, 2014

I have learned the less complicated you make your life, the quicker you achieve success. I have another level of achievement I can reach so I want to see how far I can take it.

JULY 11, 2014

Whatever you desire in life, continue to pursue that goal, and don't give up. Your goals can change based on your desires, but your genuine desires should be pursued relentlessly. When you get off track, as quickly as possible get back on track.

SEPTEMBER 23, 2014

The key to success in life is keep trying until you figure it out. Whatever IT is. Life is about the journey. Always try to learn new things and be open to change. Keep things as simple as possible. Never take life for granted; it is so precious.

NOVEMBER 8, 2014

Success is a mindset. Your brain is the most powerful part of your body. What you believe is what your brain follows. Sometimes you need to change the way you think. You do have the power to change how you think. Think big! What you focus on expands!

DECEMBER 29, 2014

Personal growth is the key to all of your success. Since I know you guys will read this one day (Connor, Izzy, Riley), I want you to hear that again: personal growth is the key to life. Always strive to grow as a person. It takes work but it is worth the effort. Leave the world a better place than you found it.

JULY 4, 2015

In life you are never too old to have fun. Parts of your life you must take seriously but sometimes losing yourself in the moment is therapeutic. Be present in the moment, have fun, and try not to stress over things that don't matter.

OCTOBER 6, 2015

I am really growing my mind, and it is really fun. You need to realize that whatever you want in life someone else likely has already accomplished. Learn from them. Think Big, Set Big Goals, and don't be afraid. Life is about the journey; it's not a race but you should immediately and aggressively pursue your dreams. Do something nice for someone every day, smile, listen, and pay attention. Think progress, not perfection.

FEBRUARY 24, 2016

Be very cautious about how you choose to spend your time. Used wisely you can achieve great things. In a battle of talent versus desire, desire usually wins. We all have the same amount of time in the day. How you use it will determine the outcome.

OCTOBER 23, 2016

When you want to do something in life or achieve something, there will be times when you get off track. Don't use that as an excuse, get going again, and get back on track. Most people just give up because they got off track, but I am telling you the more times you get back on track the closer you get to accomplishing what you want.

NOVEMBER 4, 2017

"Speak, Lord, for your servant is listening." The Lord definitely speaks to me. The key is to listen. I think we all can hear the Lord but oftentimes we choose to discount the message. Don't discount the message including those that are out of your comfort zone. The reward likely will not be instant but have no doubt there is a great reward should you choose to listen. Let the Holy Spirit do the work, just listen.

FEBRUARY 3, 2018

Momentum is powerful and doesn't happen by accident. Rarely does it happen instantly but changes in actions can begin the snowball effect. Good habits seem to lead to more good habits. Do you know what your full potential is? Do you want to find out? It takes a great commitment, but the end result will be amazing.

APRIL 10, 2018

Not everything is always going to work out as planned. Roll with the punches, and it will be easier to deal with.

JULY 16, 2018

You should do your best to remain humble and hungry. Hungry for new knowledge, hungry for personal and professional growth. Try not to hold grudges; they damage you more than the person who caused the grudge.

DECEMBER 9, 2018

Never stop learning and always be curious. Don't ever think you are better than someone else; you have no idea what they have gone through. Be humble and be thankful.

FEBRUARY 13, 2019

I don't like being in a slump, but when you really think about it, no one is on all the time. They may appear that way, but it's just not reality. When you are in a slump, pick your head up and move forward. What's the alternative? Digress and fall deeper into the slump? No thanks!

NOVEMBER 7, 2019

Character = your ability to stick with whatever you decided to do long after the emotion/excitement of the decision wears off.

DECEMBER 22, 2019

When you put your intentions out into the world, followed up with action in the direction of those intentions, you might surprise yourself with the results.

JANUARY 30, 2020

I am working on a breakthrough and I will admit that doubt sometimes creeps in. I believe the difference between good and great is your ability to be aware when doubt is present, then proceed regardless. Confidence will resurface and when doubt tries to creep back in, punch it in the face because you got this!

FINAL LESSON

Let's see if I can land this plane. This is your captain speaking. I'd like to thank you for traveling the Martin express today. We hope you've enjoyed your ride with us today. It has been the greatest joy of my life to be your captain. I want to thank our passengers today for allowing me to live a great life, a full life. My hope for you as you travel to your next destination is that you too experience the joy you have given me. I love you, Martin family, more than you will ever know. Until next time. I can't wait!

This book was an experiment for me, and while it might seem like I have everything figured out in life, I do *not*. I am crystal clear that my family is my top priority, but I have so much more to learn. When I decided to write the book, I had no idea the challenges and benefits that writing would provide. As I approach the finish line of becoming an author, I can't help but realize that the finish line looks more like a starting line. I am not sure what my next race will look like but make no mistake: I plan on registering.

I am proud of what you have in your hands because I pushed myself beyond my comfort zone, I went *all in*. In reflection, I have realized that I am living this book. The words written aren't just words. They are my core convictions, values, and beliefs. This book is who I am.

Here are some of the things I learned through the writing process.

1. **Anyone can write a book**. I recommend a coach like Azul Terronez, but if I can write a book, anyone can write a book.

2. **I learned how to take a punch to the gut.** Remember, this is actually my second book, since the first attempt will never be published.

3. **Consistency.** This is a word that haunts me, but writing a book requires it. Consistency is required for success in life and definitely for writing a book. I should have written a chapter about this word because it's that important.

4. **Others reap the benefits.** My children watched me go through this process and Riley has already begun writing her first book. I am most excited about this benefit because my kids know that if Dad can do it, they can do it.

5. **What you tell yourself matters.** The entire time I am writing, my brain is paying attention to what I am saying. Writing can transform your brain. It starts to respond to the message you want it to receive. It leads me to a question: what do I want next in my life? Should I write about it?

6. **I am just getting started.** After forty-three trips around the sun, I believe I have barely scratched the surface of my own potential.

7. **Start early.** When the sun rises, so does my family, so I had to make writing a priority very early in the morning, usually around 5:30 a.m.

8. **Lessons learned.** Every lesson I have learned while writing this book I will now apply to different areas of my life.

9. **Ideas to actions.** Take an idea and put it into action, even if it takes five years.

MEET THE AUTHOR

J ASON MARTIN HAS no experience as a writer and does not consider himself an academic. Truth be told, he failed copyediting in college and has no business writing a book. However, now that the book has been published, he will absolutely consider himself an author.

Jason also considers himself a meteorologist as well as a doctor. He has no formal training in either subject;

he simply believes that he can predict your medical condition better than the doctor. As a predictor of weather, he makes his own snowfall predictions that he feels outperform those of local meteorologists. Jason also considers himself an athlete, playing old man basketball several times per week.

Jason's family will absolutely confirm his beliefs and they will also absolutely confirm he has no idea what he is talking about. His self-proclaimed titles might seem a bit suspect, as they are frequently questioned by the Martin family. His family often scratches their heads, wondering how his confidence came to be. However, one thing they never question is Jason's love for them.

Jason's family is his number-one priority in life, and nothing is more important to him than the moments and memories they create together.

Jason is a husband and father of four children. He and his wife, Jennifer Spatz-Martin, reside in Alexandria, Virginia, with three human children. The fourth sibling in the Martin family is Scooby the dog—a.k.a., Mister Furry. Jason's approach to life is quite simple. He wants to be the best husband and father he can be—that's how he defines success.

Jason attended the University of South Carolina where he met his lovely bride, Jennifer. Jason and Jennifer consider themselves proud "Cocks." To clarify,

Cocky is the official mascot of the University of South Carolina. Jason was a former sports anchor and now runs one of the most successful real estate teams in Washington, DC.

Jason believes in personal and professional growth, self-development, and achieving things you never thought possible, like writing a book. Before we set sail, you should know that Jason also considers himself a captain. "This is your captain speaking. Welcome aboard the Martin Express, where today you will learn everything I always wanted you to know. I am grateful for you taking the time to read my first book."

You can reach Jason at
jason@jasonmartingroup.com

I would appreciate your feedback on
what chapters helped you most, and what you
would like to see in future books.

If you enjoyed this book and found it helpful,
please leave a REVIEW on Amazon.

Visit us at
TODAYYOUCHOOSE.COM
where you can sign up for email updates.

Connect with me directly by email:
JASON@JASONMARTINGROUP.COM

Thank you!